D0853131

LIVES&
LEGACIES

Joan of Arc

ALSO IN THE LIVES & LEGACIES SERIES:

Duke Ellington

Frantz Fanon

Frida Kahlo

Rumi

SERIES EDITOR: BARBARA LEAH ELLIS

SIOBHAN NASH-MARSHALL

Joan of Arc

A Spiritual Biography

A Crossroad Book
The Crossroad Publishing Company
New York

The Crossroad Publishing Company
370 Lexington Avenue, New York, NY 10017

First published in 1999 by The Crossroad Publishing Company

Copyright © 1999 by Siobhan Nash-Marshall

LIBRARY OF CONGRESS CATALOGING-IN-PUBLICATION DATA
Nash-Marshall, Siobhan
Joan of Arc : a spiritual biography / written by Siobhan Nash-Marshall.
p. cm. – (Lives & Legacies)
Includes bibliographical references.
ISBN 0-8245-2350-4 (hc)
1. Joan, of Arc, Saint, 1412–1431. 2. Spirituality—France—History—
Middle Ages, 600–1500. 3. Christian women saints—France
Biography. I. Title.
DC103.N28   1999
944' .026' 092—dc21
[B]   99-38952 CIP

Printed in the United States of America
Set in Janson
Designed by SCRIBES Editorial
Cover design by Kaeser and Wilson Design Ltd.

1 2 3 4 5 6 7 8 9 10 03 02 01 00 99

to Joan
Honi soit qui mal y pense

CONTENTS

Joan of Arc

Joan of Arc standing with her battle standard in hand, by the alter in Rheims Cathedral during Charles's coronation.
(Courtesy Giraudon/Art Resource, NY)

1

The Inquisitor and the Maid

Be careful, you who call yourself my judge! Be careful
about what you are doing, because my quest does come
from God, and you are taking a terrible risk!

—*Joan of Arc*

THE ORDEAL WAS FINALLY coming to an end. After a year of
imprisonment, a four month trial, an abjuration and a counter-
abjuration, Joan of Arc was to be burnt at the stake. The *Vieux
Marché*, the old marketplace at Rouen, was swarming with people.
It was the second time in less than a week that a crowd had gathered to see her, and everyone there knew that there could be no
third. A relapsed "heretic" could know no end other than death.

Escorted by what eyewitnesses claim were some eight hundred soldiers armed with axes and swords, the death cart bearing
Joan rolled into the square where there was an enormous scaffold
with a massive plaster stake bearing the sign: "*Joan called the
Virgin, liar, pernicious, seducer of the people, diviner, superstitious, blas-
phemer of God, defamer of the faith of Jesus Christ, braggart, idola-
trous, cruel, dissolute, invoker of devils, apostate, schismatic, and
heretic.*" Wood had already been piled around the stake.

Three other wooden platforms loomed above the square.
Waiting for her on the first one, lavishly decorated with tapes-
tries, were her accusers—the members of the ecclesiastical court
who were about to excommunicate her. The bailiff of Rouen and
his entourage—the secular authorities, who were called upon to

sentence Joan to death and carry out the execution—were on the second platform. It was adjacent to the first. Nicholas Midi of the University of Paris, who was one of the court assessors, stood on the third platform. It was somewhat removed from the first two platforms and askew with respect to them. What ensued was the slow and meticulous dance of public death.

Joan was made to dismount from the cart, climb up the steps of the third platform, and join Midi. When she had taken her proper place, the once Rector of the Parisian University plunged into a sermon on the iniquities and infectious nature of heresy. "When one member suffers," he began, "all suffer with it."

Ten thousand pairs of eyes were glued to his platform, caught, one imagines, in the unfolding of the ritual rather than in the content of the sermon per se. One pair of eyes paid careful attention to his words. They were those of Pierre Cauchon, the bishop of Beauvais and the chief Inquisitor at Joan's trial, who sat on the ecclesiastical platform. He was waiting for his cue. Cauchon was patient that day. He had to be. Midi was a long-winded academic, who was determined to put up a particularly powerful performance for the occasion. He spoke for a full hour.

But Cauchon could afford to be patient on that day. He had won his war; and as most winners would, he probably enjoyed the fact that his victory celebration was long. Cauchon was a vain man. As the "distinguished doctor" finally drew his sermon to a close, he slowly rose. It was nine o'clock, and his turn had come.

All eyes shifted to the Inquisitor as he read her sentence: "like a dog that returns to its vomit" Joan had relapsed, she had returned to her heretical ways. He therefore excommunicated her—"cut [her] off like a leprous limb from the Church"—and handed her over to the secular authorities, who would deal with her as they saw fit. He "hoped they would be merciful." This phrase was customary. It was just one of the many steps in the dance. Everyone there knew how secular authorities dealt with excommunicated heretics. They sentenced them to death at the stake.

On the platform opposite Cauchon's, Midi then turned to Joan and repeated the conclusion of Cauchon's sentence. "Go in peace," he told her. "The Church can no longer protect you and delivers you up to the secular arm." This was the cue for the men waiting on the last platform: the secular authorities. The bailiff of Rouen stood up and called upon two sergeants to seize Joan, accompany her down the steps, and over to him.

Joan was dragged through the jeering crowd over to the bailiff's platform and stood in front of the bailiff for some time awaiting her sentence. But the bailiff had somehow forgotten his lines. He delivered no official death sentence. After some discussion, he finally raised his hand, called out his orders—"Take her away! Take her away!"—and had her hastily, too hastily, escorted on to the scaffold, and up to the executioner. The ecclesiastical authorities then rose and began to depart from the scene. The matter was officially out of their hands.

Once Joan had climbed the stairs of the scaffold, the executioner removed the white sorceress's bonnet—which it is said she was made to wear up to that time—and replaced it with a tall paper cap, which read: "*heretic, relapsed, apostate, idolatress.*" He then hoisted her up to the massive plaster stake, chained her to it, and lit the wood.

Like the bailiff, whose steps had faltered in that fateful dance—he was later reprimanded for not having issued the death sentence—the executioner, Geoffrey Thérage, was not altogether pleased with his performance that morning. After it was over, he complained bitterly about the cruelty of Joan's execution. Her stake, it seems, was too high for him to be able to "reach her and hasten her end"—a part of the ritual that was not meant for public eyes, and which made death at the stake infinitely less cruel. He was not even able to place a faggot of green wood, whose smoke would have killed Joan before the flames, at her feet.

Joan did not go to the stake with a fight. She had shot her last arrow sometime earlier, while she was still in her prison cell, when she told Bishop Cauchon that he alone was responsible for her death and would be held so by God. He had broken his word, and had not sent her to an ecclesiastical prison. It is reported that Joan listened "peaceably" to the sermon and sentence, and broke down only when she was to be delivered to the secular authorities. It was then that she let everyone see her fear of death and feel the weight of it. She fell to her knees and asked everyone in the square to pray for her. She specifically asked priests each to say a mass for her. She forgave everyone involved in her death and asked them to forgive her. She spoke for a half hour.

Many of the witnesses—including some members of the ecclesiastical court who condemned her—wept openly at her words. But Joan was to be cut short by the English soldiers waiting in the square. "Priest," they called out, "Are you going to have us dine here?" As Joan made for the stake, she was heard to ask, "Rouen, shall I die here?" But as she still hoped to escape the gruesome death that awaited her, she also was fully aware of the consequences of her death. She quickly responded to her own question, "Ah, Rouen, Rouen, I fear that you will suffer for my death!"

Jean Massieu, the court usher who accompanied Joan to the stake, said that she then asked him and Isambard de la Pierre— a Dominican member of the ecclesiastical court who was also at her side—for a cross. An English soldier quickly made one for her, while Isambard went to the nearby Church of Saint-Sauveur to get the processional crucifix which she might see through the flames and smoke. Joan seized the little cross from the Englishman, kissed it, and clutched it to her breast. Isambard returned just in time for Joan to embrace the crucifix. Her hands were then bound, she was chained to the stake, and the fire was lit. From the fire, she was heard to call repeatedly upon God to rescue her. She called upon Michael the Archangel, St. Margaret, and St. Catherine to come to her assistance. She called for some holy water. Finally, she yelled "Jesus" several times in a loud voice and died.

Witnesses claim that once the executioner was sure that Joan had died, he briefly pushed the fire back from her naked corpse. Joan's accusers felt that it was important for everyone who had gathered in the square to see both that Joan was just an ordinary woman and that she had indeed died. Once the fire had died, her ashes were gathered and thrown into the Seine. It is rumored that her heart would not burn.

There are many things about Joan of Arc's death that have puzzled people for centuries. Why exactly did the Church condemn her? The answer seems simple enough: Joan was burnt at the stake because the Inquisition believed her to be a heretic. This is what her trial record indicates; it is what death at the stake indicates; it is what the inscription on the stake indicates. And yet, as it is with so many things in Joan's life, the simple answer somehow does not account for all of the facts. If Joan was indeed simply condemned for heresy, why was she given the sacraments the very morning of the day she died? To be precise, how could Pierre Cauchon, the bishop of Beauvais and Joan's chief Inquisitor, have allowed Joan to partake in what the Catholic Church holds to be the most sacred of all things, if he held that she was a heretic? Cauchon had withheld the sacraments from Joan for five months up to that point. He had not even allowed her to receive them in the days following her abjuration and preceding her recantation, even though Joan herself claims that he had promised to give them to her—if she abjured. And yet, on the morning of her execution, he allowed her to have what he would not grant her till that time. Why?

The question of the sacraments must have also crossed the mind of Martin Ladvenu, the Dominican monk who was in Joan's cell in the very early morning of the day she died. It was he who had Joan's last request taken to the bishop. Ladvenu had heard Joan's last confession that morning. Indeed, he had heard it twice. And as she had so many times before, Joan begged to receive the Eucharist—the body of Christ. Ladvenu did not know how to deal with her request. Her confession must have convinced him that she was in the "proper state" of soul to receive it. But the Eucharist had been denied Joan so many times by the Inquisitor—and what is more, Joan was about to be officially excommunicated—that Ladvenu did not know if granting her request was the proper thing to do. So he consulted his superior, Cauchon.

Cauchon himself was not quite sure about the proper course of action. After some deliberation—and consultation—he responded, "Give her everything she asks." And so Ladvenu did, despite some astounding difficulties that suggest that no one had thought of giving Joan the sacrament at all: the Eucharist was carried at first into Joan's cell in what the Dominican monk felt was such a highly irreverent manner that he had to send it back.

Cauchon may have finally consented to give Joan the sacraments to appease his conscience, or he may have thought that Joan was innocent. Perhaps he took the sacraments lightly. Or he may have thought it best to put the matter into God's hands. It could also be that some event had taken place that made him indifferent as to whether Joan received the sacraments or not. These are all possibilities; all of them make the "heresy" charge very suspicious indeed. It is noteworthy that the point was brought up at Joan's rehabilitation trial.[1]

Joan was executed as a relapsed heretic, because she was found dressed in men's clothing three days after she had sworn never to wear men's clothing again. What makes that event so strange is that it would have been virtually impossible for Joan to put men's clothing on at that time unless, of course, she was helped. Joan was in her prison cell when the change of clothes took place. And while she was in her prison cell, she was not only heavily guarded—there were at least three guards with her in her cell at all times—she also wore leg irons and was chained by the waist to a large wooden block. It is also unclear where the clothes she ended up wearing came from. The one clear thing is that Joan could not have had access to them unless someone had given them to her.

Some witnesses stated that Joan claimed to have awakened on that fateful day to discover that her dress had disappeared and been replaced by men's clothing and, as such, that the only clothes she could have put on were men's. When the Inquisitor questioned her on the point, however, Joan claimed to have been the only person responsible for the change in clothes.

Did Joan claim responsibility for the change in order to bring an impossible situation to an end? It is possible. It is rumored that Joan was molested in those three days that elapsed between her abjuration and her "relapse." And above and beyond rumors, which may or may not be true, what is beyond doubt is that Joan's situation had become unbearable. "She said that she preferred to do her penitence once and for all, by dying, to enduring her pain in prison."[2] Joan's accepting the responsibility for her changing her attire is thus perfectly understandable. This does not, however, change the fact that she could not have returned to male dress through her own will alone. Someone must have helped her change.

It is curious that Joan was in an English prison and guarded by men in the first place. Secular prisons were not the places in which the Church commonly detained self-confessed heretics in the Middle Ages. The medieval Church had its own prisons for confessed heretics. They were usually convents or monasteries, depending upon the gender of the heretic. It was common practice for female heretics to have female jailers, and male heretics to have male ones. Joan knew this, and even was given promise to be sent to an ecclesiastical prison if she abjured. Her comments at her "relapse" show that she had expected that prison to be a convent. She claimed she would not have changed clothes if the Inquisitor had kept his word—if she had been "sent to a church prison with a woman for companion."

Execution of Joan of Arc, depicted as a more conventionally feminine martyr with long blond hair. (Courtesy Giraudon/Art Resource, NY)

Joan of Arc by Rossetti. French national heroine, the proceedings of Joan's original trial were annulled in 1456, and she was cannonized in 1920. (Courtesy Tate Gallery, London/Art Resource, NY)

And what of that mysterious abjuration in the cemetery of St. Ouen? There are at least two inexplicable things about that event. The first is Joan's laugh; the second regards the document Joan actually did sign. Eyewitnesses claim that after having been pressured by the Inquisitor (he had actually had a stake built for the occasion and had an executioner present, cart and all, in order to terrify Joan into a confession) and after having been told that she could not call upon the pope to judge her case (which was not true), Joan was presented with a document to sign. It was an abjuration. If she signed, she was told, her sentence would be reduced from death at the stake to life imprisonment; if she did not, she would be burnt immediately at the stake. A member of the court read the content of the document; Joan was illiterate. After having called upon her saints to protect her, Joan laughed, picked up the quill, and signed the document.

Joan's reaction is strange to say the least. After having fought against the Inquisitor for months without giving him anything substantial with which to condemn her, she agreed to sign a confession. Did she not know that she was signing her death warrant? And above all, why did she laugh as she signed her earthly damnation? What is more mysterious yet is the content of the document Joan did sign. The lengthy document on record cannot possibly be the few lines that witnesses claim to have seen her sign. Witnesses claim that the document she signed was very short—that it was as long as an *Our Father*—and generic. The document on record, on the other hand, is long and articulate.

Joan was burnt at the stake for having "returned" to her "heretical" ways, for having "foresworn" what she had sworn at the cemetery of St. Ouen. She was burnt at the stake for being a *relapsed* heretic. The content of the original document she signed therefore plays a central role in her death: It spells out what Joan had sworn not to do. But the Inquisitor felt that it was necessary to substitute the original document.

The key events that marked Joan's path to the scaffold—her "abjuration" and her counter-abjuration—are not the only odd things about her end. The juridical events of the last months of her life—her trial, her imprisonment, and her double condemnation—are just as strange, yet what are more conspicuous in their absence, are the key events that did not take place. Joan's allies—her king, the king she had put on the throne—did not save her once she had fallen into enemy hands. Her allies had ample time to do so; Joan had been in prison for a full year before she was put to death. King Charles could easily have ransomed her during the first six months of that year. It was probably even expected of him; ransoming prisoners was customary, after all.

The mysteries shrouding the slow end of Joan's life all point to a sinister plot behind Joan's death. Someone wanted her to suffer a painful public death, and that someone wanted to make sure that the death was perceived as an act of God's—or one which was in accord with his will. This explains the discrepancies between the public and private treatment of Joan on the day that she died: the fact that she was privately given the sacraments and publicly excommunicated and burnt at the stake. It also accounts for the incredible machinations involved in getting Joan to the stake and helps to explain the carefully orchestrated execution.

And there is no mistaking the fact that Joan's death was the quest of the Inquisitor and the English crown. Pierre Cauchon, for whatever reason, wanted to see Joan condemned and executed as a heretic. He pursued that goal for many months and with great zeal. He was even forced to bend a few very important rules here and there to ensure the outcome. Nor was his a lonely passion. The English crown and its representatives were just as eager to see her chained to the stake. Not only did they lay out enormous amounts of money to guarantee that she was burnt, but they could not even wait for the sentence of a secular judge to light the fire under her feet when she finally was executed. Their haste made her execution illegal.

The quest of the Inquisitor and the English crown was not merely to get Joan out of the way. Had it been, it could easily have been accomplished through simpler means. There were such things as assassins even in the fifteenth century. Their quest was to have her publicly denounced, shamed, and exposed. Their mission was for the public to witness her die as a fraud. The earl of Warwick put the point succinctly: "The king—the English king—does not wish for anything in the world that she [Joan] die a natural death. For he holds her dear, having dearly bought her." That statement was made after Joan had abjured. The English feared that Joan had escaped their grip with her abjuration. One could not execute a *penitent* heretic who had given herself to the Church.

Why it was so important to Cauchon and the English crown that Joan be publicly executed has been long debated. So has the question of who Joan was and what her significance really was. Edward Lucie-Smith stated in 1976 that by the 1920s, over twelve thousand books had been written about Joan.[3] No doubt that number has grown dramatically since then. Joan has had a powerful hold on minds and imaginations since she first stepped into the public light in 1429, a young girl from "the marshes of Lorraine," who claimed to have been "sent by God to liberate France from the English."

There is little consensus with regard to anything at all concerning Joan, her significance, or her role in history. There are those who attempt to minimize her significance. They point out that her time in the spotlight was very brief and her power very limited. After all, she only really held the royal ear for three months—from May to July 1430—and when she did, she did not "really have much clout." They point out that she was never the official leader of the royal armies of France—d'Alençon and Dunois—and as such that she did not decide which campaigns were to be fought, or when and how they were to be. Nor, in their opinion, could she have been a real *chef de guerre*. They feel that Joan was not capable of making military decisions. She was a farm girl, the claim goes, who was born in an age in which noblemen were the beginning and end of all war-making. Nor was there a West Point that she might have attended to learn how to wage war. Their conclusion, therefore, is that Joan was simply a mystic—an ecstatic mascot for the royal army of France in those very brief months of her ascendancy.[4]

There are, of course, variations on this interpretation. Some biographers have added that Joan, like the *Forelle* of the song made famous by Schubert's quintet, was also caught up in a net of political intrigue, which was beyond her understanding and scope, and which eventually pulled her down.[5] Thus, they add political to her military ignorance. There are also many others who would like to give Joan more than just a central role in the French victory of the Hundred Years' War and in the birth of the French nation. She has been portrayed as a mystical savior of France and of its pre-Christian pagan rites;[6] a conscious proto-type of feminine heroism;[7] a forerunner of the communist revolution;[8] and all manner of odd things.[9]

The lack of consensus about Joan is not as odd as it seems. Joan was a *quester*: an individual who had a powerful sense of purpose, an extraordinary mission. One characteristic common to all questers, is that they become their quests, in some sense. Socrates was the gadfly of Athens, Aristotle her philosopher, St. Francis was God's troubadour, St. Thomas his scientist. Questers live for their quests and see no life outside of their quests. Their spectacular focus is what gives them their strength. It is also what makes their lives so singularly joyful.

Once Joan understood what she was called to do—that it was up to her to free France—she pursued her quest with extraordinary single-mindedness. She knew what she had to do, and that it would be done: All she needed was tenacity, courage and faith. And that is precisely what she had. Witnesses at her rehabilitation trial recount that she fretted like a "woman who was about to give birth," when it came to fulfilling her quest. She literally laid siege to those people whom she had to convince to aid her until they consented to do what she demanded of them. Her zeal on the battlefield was exemplary. And it is precisely because it was that the Anglo-Burgundians managed to capture her. She was part of the rearguard of her retreating ambushed forces in that last fateful skirmish at Compiègne and was thus outside the town when its gates were shut.

Nor is her passion at her trial any less breathtaking. Pitted against people who were far older and more experienced than she, Joan managed to stave off the stake for months, despite the incredible physical and psychological hardships which she had to endure. Her death was just one last demonstration of her passion. She had the strength to "relapse" and to claim responsibility for it, despite the fact that she knew it meant death—and was terrified of it.

The fact that questers become their quests is what makes them such controversial figures. They simply defy categorization. Quests are extraordinary missions, and the extraordinary cannot be defined through ordinary means. To define Joan simply as a warrior or simply as a person of extraordinary faith is to misunderstand Joan. Joan was both things at once. But how does one define that combination? It defies categories. It defies logic. Joan is a scandal, in the original sense of the word. It is no wonder, then, that there have been so many vastly different interpretations of Joan's life.

Since questers have extraordinary missions they often use extraordinary means to accomplish their missions. Their quests often lead them to challenge the status quo, customs, and mores. Joan, who was in this respect no different from thousands of other people whose lives were missions, defied many customs in pursuit of her quest. Joan could hardly have changed the course of history if she had let herself be bothered by the unwritten medieval rule that held that noblemen alone could be *chefs de guerre*. Nor could she have led and lived with an army if she had attempted to accommodate social mores.

The defiance of custom leads many people to concentrate on the means the questers use to fulfill their callings—rather than on the quester's quest, and makes them misunderstand both the quester and his quest. The Inquisitor, for example, could not understand why Joan insisted on wearing men's clothing. It was blasphemous, he claimed. The matter came up time and time again her trial. Joan, on the other hand, could not understand why he considered her clothing so important. Her clothing was a secondary thing, she responded time and time again. Joan died because she returned to men's garb. The Inquisitor took it to be a sign of her relapse.

Contemporary feminists often set their sights exclusively on Joan's dismissal of custom. And it is for this reason that they can make her out to be a precursor of contemporary feminism. They can interpret her dismissal of custom as a sign of her will to affirm her sex. Others set their sights on other unusual things in Joan's behavior—there are plenty anyone can point to—and make her out to be a shaman, a communist, a heretic, and so forth. Hence the plethora of interpretations.

Finally, what makes questers so difficult to deal with is their extraordinary passion. And passion tends to engender passion. It is very difficult to look upon questers without seeing them through the respect, admiration, incredulity, or perhaps even disgust that they elicit. It is very difficult to think dispassionately of a young girl in armor whose zeal on the battlefield stirred a defeated people to rise and throw off the yoke of foreign domination. It is also very difficult to think dispassionately of an eighteen-year-old peasant girl in a red dress who knocked on the door of the high and mighty to convince them that God had sent her to crown the king.

2

Domrémy

> It was my mother who taught me
> the *Ave Maria, Pater Noster,* and *Credo.*
>
> —*Joan of Arc*

JOAN WAS BORN IN THE VILLAGE of Domrémy, which is in the province of Vaucouleurs, in what scholars presume was 1412. Her birthday is celebrated on January 6. Like 1412, however, the latter is just a conventional date. There is no way of knowing the exact date of Joan's birth. The Middle Ages put no great worth in chronological exactness of this sort. The year on record is drawn from Joan's own testimony. When the Inquisitor questioned her on the point, she declared that she thought she was 19, and that was in 1431. As for the day, it is given by Perceval de Boulainvilliers, one of Charles of Valois's chamberlains, who was eager to show that Joan was earmarked for greatness from the first.[1]

January 6 is an important religious holiday, and to the medieval mind, which saw meaning in all sorts of different things, it made perfect sense to claim not only that Joan had to be born on an important day but also that that specific day had to be January 6. Whatever her contemporaries thought of her, they immediately acknowledged that Joan was someone important and therefore felt that it was a necessary tribute to assign an important birthday to her. January 6 is Epiphany, the day in which Christians celebrate the acknowledgement of the kingship of Christ. Thus it

Statue of Joan of Arc. Also called the Maid of Orléans, her career lent itself to many legends, and she has been represented in much art and literature. (Courtesy Giraudon/Art Resource, NY)

Below: Birthplace of Joan of Arc. (Courtesy SEF/Art Resource, NY)

made sense to claim that that specific day had to be the day of Joan's birth. Joan's mission, after all, was to make both England and France acknowledge Charles of Valois's kingship over France. The point would not have been lost in the Middle Ages.

The place of Joan's birth is in a sense just as vague as the time of her birth. Domrémy was a border town in the fifteenth century. It is on the Meuse, which at that time was the traditional border between France and the Holy Roman Empire. This made the proprietorship of the town rather hazy. Border towns have that special trait still today. In the Middle Ages, however, the haziness was heightened by the fact that borders shifted. This meant that it was never altogether clear if the little town was French, or whether it belonged to the duchy of Lorraine, which technically owed allegiance to the Holy Roman Emperor.[2]

To make matters worse, Domrémy also happened to be on a series of secondary borders within France: those that separated Champagne, the duchy of Bar, and the Barrois Mouvant, a part of the duchy of Bar that had been ceded to the royal house of France in 1335. It was also very close to Burgundy. This meant that above and beyond whatever larger property disputes there may have been regarding Domrémy, no one in France was quite sure to whom the town belonged.

Despite their vagueness, or possibly even because of it, both the time and place of Joan's birth play a significant role in her story. The time is particularly important. In the 1410s, the Hundred Years' War, which had already been raging and lulling for over seventy years, took a drastic turn which was to lead the king of France to grant the inheritance of the throne of France to the king of England in 1420. The major events of the decade were the battle of Agincourt, which took place in 1415, in which Henry V of England literally slaughtered the French, and the allegiance, which the French duke of Burgundy decided to strike with the English crown in 1417.

France and England have always had complicated relations. They conquered and reconquered each other's lands for centuries. The political muddle began in 1066, when William the duke of Normandy won the battle of Hastings and grabbed the English throne. What made that event such a politically complicated affair was that it jumbled the statuses of both England and Normandy. William had, after all, sworn fealty to the king of France. He was a French duke. Technically, one could as such have argued that his conquest of England made that land a French fief. This was, however, just a technicality. William the Conqueror had no intention of handing England over to the king of France after he had personally taken the time and energy to conquer it. So he quickly had himself crowned king of England in order to avert any possible doubt on the matter.

There would have been nothing politically complicated about that event either, had William been content with his English crown and given up his French duchy, but giving up the duchy of Normandy was the farthest thing from William's mind. He had inherited the duchy, and it was an important one. Nor, however, could he annex Normandy to his own kingdom of England—it was a part of the kingdom of France. So William compromised: he kept the duchy without annexing it to England. This was very strange indeed. It made William, who was a king on one side of the English Channel, a vassal on the other, and it made the duchy of Normandy the possession of both the king of England and the king of France.

In the years that followed, things became more, rather than less, complicated. In 1152 Henry Plantagenet, William's great-grandson and heir, married Eleanor of Aquitaine, who was not only the queen of France by marriage but also the heiress of the duchy of Aquitaine, which was an enormous part of France, and a very wealthy one at that. When Eleanor married Henry—who was eleven years her junior—she naturally ceased to be the queen of France (her marriage to Louis VII was annulled) but she did not cease to be the duchess of Aquitaine; she had inherited that title and the lands that went with it. Nor did Henry Plantagenet, who happened to be the count of Anjou as well as the duke of Normandy, give up his titles or the lands that went with them when he was crowned king of England in 1154. Actually, he did a bit of conquering of his own: he added Brittany to his long list of French properties. As a result, in the mid-twelfth century more than half of France belonged to the king of England—who was technically speaking the vassal of the king of France.

These Anglo-French relations naturally were the source of many wars and counterwars between the French and the English kings. For the French kings could not have vassals who were more powerful than they, and the English kings were loath to give up their French lands or pay homage to the kings of France. But kings are royals as well as generals. And royals intermarry. This complicated matters enormously. As things turned out, in 1328 when the last direct male descendent of the king of France died, Edward III of England had at least as strong a claim to the throne of France as did the proclaimed heir to that throne, Philip of Valois, who quickly had himself crowned and anointed king of France in order to forestall a war.

Edward had no intention of really laying a serious claim to the throne of France. He had other more important battles to attend to and, what is more, coronations—anointings, above all—were a sacred thing in the Middle Ages. Events, however, rather pushed him to do so. In 1337, King Philip confiscated King Edward's French properties. His excuse was that Edward had given refuge to his archenemy Robert of Artois. Excuses or not, however, Edward did not take kindly to the confiscation. So he declared himself king of France and decided to fight for his claim. This was the beginning of the Hundred Years' War. Edward sent his first army over to France in 1339.

Edward III won many important battles against the French. In 1346 he literally crushed the French army at Crécy; in 1356 he did the same thing at Poitiers. But he was never crowned king of France. Despite his victories, he had not been able to oust King Philip. So his heirs took up the fight, and sent troops to France as often as they could; and the war over the French throne lingered on, and on. Not that it was a constant war. It was a medieval one, and that meant that the fighting took place at spurts—and lasted as long as the royal purse did. This did not make the war any less devastating. For when the royal purse ran out, the disbanded armies often turned into marauders, who ravaged the French countryside, looting and terrorizing farmers, monks, peasants and travelers.

Joan was born when the Hundred Years' War was on the verge of blotting France out altogether. The danger was not just political. The war itself had taken an enormous toll on the people of France and their land. It had ravished their countryside and their numbers. France's population literally halved in the seventy odd years that separated the beginning of the Hundred Years' War and Joan's birth. War was not the only cause of the appalling number of deaths in France in those years. Black Death, famine, and poverty had also left their marks. But the war was definitely a major contributing factor in the destruction.

Not only was Joan born in the worst of times, but she was born right in the lion's den. Domrémy was dangerously close to being a war zone in the early fifteenth century. The little village happened to be near the crossroads between two crucial medieval trade routes: the one that went from Basel to the major towns in Champagne and the one that went from Trier to Lyon. This made Domrémy the sort of town for which those greater powers, who could lay claim to the town, might sooner or later fight. Trade routes were an important source of revenue in the Middle Ages.

Situated as it was on the borders of Champagne, Bar, and the royal lands, Domrémy was a sort of powder keg around the time of Joan's birth. The various people who could lay claim to the

Charles the Mad

In the late fourteenth century, Charles VI was crowned king of France. Modern psychologists claim that Charles was schizophrenic.[3] The bouts of royal madness were serious, recurrent, and long. Charles killed four of his attendants during his first fit in 1392, and had forty-three fits after that first one. They lasted anywhere from three to nine months. This meant that someone had to take up Charles's royal responsibilities for him during these bouts of madness.

This triggered a power war within France. Charles's kinsmen—his brother, Louis of Orléans and his first cousin John the Fearless of Burgundy—each thought that he was the best man to take over for their mad king.

Their personal power struggle came to a dramatic end in 1407 when Louis, who returning home after a luxurious dinner with his sister-in-law, Queen Isabeau, was murdered by John the Fearless. It was replaced by a civil war in France.

The count of Armagnac rallied men to his (and the king's) side in order to call the duke of Burgundy to order. Burgundy, on the other hand, called men to his side and defense. It was thus that the nobility of France was divided into the Armagnac and the Burgundian factions.

In 1417, the duke of Burgundy, who had his own private plan for power, decided to foster a secret allegiance with the king of England and back his claim to the throne of France. The secret pact became public in 1419, when John the Fearless himself was murdered by henchmen sent by the mad king Charles's son, Charles the dauphin. The Hundred Years' War then became a civil war, with the Anglo-Burgundians fighting the Armagnacs, who were loyal to the royal house of France.

In 1420, the mad king signed a treaty with Henry V of England which gave the English king both the right of succession to the throne of France and a French wife: Charles's daughter. Rumors were spread about the dauphin's legitimacy. Queen Isabeau herself let it be believed that her son was her dead brother-in-law Louis of Orléans's bastard.

village were the protagonists of the Hundred Years' War itself. Champagne was solidly in Anglo-Burgundian hands at that time, as were the duchy of Bar, and the neighboring duchy of Burgundy. The royal house of France, which could also lay claim to the town, on the other hand, was clearly Armagnac.

Then there was Domrémy's political allegiance. The inhabitants of the village were staunchly Armagnac, despite the fact that a large portion of the lands that surrounded their little town was solidly in Burgundian hands. Even the children of Domrémy were involved in the politics of the day. At her trial, Joan recounted that the children from Domrémy were involved in occasional skirmishes with the Burgundians from the nearby town of Maxey, and came back with bloody noses. She also told her judges that she only knew of one dissenter among the villagers of Domrémy, one person who did not believe that Charles of Valois was the true heir to the French throne, and added that "she would most gladly have lopped off his head, God willing."[4] This meant that the little town was hemmed in by enemies who clearly wanted to "convert" it, and weren't afraid of using the sword to do so.

As such, war was no stranger to Domrémy in Joan's time. It was a matter of course for most of the French in her day. The Hundred Years' War had been going on for almost a hundred years by the time she was born, as Joan herself had the chance to point out to the Inquisitor. In her childhood, however, it had boiled down to occupation, taxes, and perhaps even discontent, in much of northeastern France. In many respects, the Treaty of Troyes, which gave the English king the French throne, simply formalized a reality with which quite a few northern Frenchmen had already come to terms. Domrémy (and Vaucouleurs) were singled out in this respect. They constituted one of the rare remaining hot beds in what had substantially become an Anglo-Burgundian fief.

Skirmishes and military excursions then were not all that unusual for the little town. Joan herself recalled at her trial that she was called upon on different occasions to bring her father's cattle to the Domrémy's stronghold, the Island, when the town feared encroaching soldiers. The villagers did not always get their cattle to safety. In 1425, an Anglo-Burgundian raiding party made off with Domrémy's cattle. It also plundered and burnt the village while it was at it. In 1428, as Joan herself recalled, they did it again. During that incursion of Burgundian soldiers, she told her judges, she and her family—with, other witnesses claim, the entire town of Domrémy—were forced to flee to the town of Neufchâteau in Lorraine and stay there for about fifteen days. Their church and crops were burnt when they got back.

Joan was the fourth of the five children of Jacques d'Arc and Isabelle Romée. Her parents were farmers. They were neither serfs, nor peasants, nor paupers. Nor were they desperate. Jacques d'Arc was a rather well off, enterprising, and respected man. He was a small landowner, who was the *doyen* of Domrémy in 1423, which meant that he was responsible for the town's defense and levied the town's taxes. He was also called upon on different occasions to represent the town's interest at parleys with noble authorities; it was he who signed the lease for the Island—the stronghold in which the townspeople kept their cattle during Burgundian raids.

Jacques's political roles give us the measure of the man. Jacques d'Arc was not from Domrémy at all. He moved to the little town from his native Ceffonds in Champagne[5] after he married Joan's mother. What this means, of course, is that he had to win the respect of his townsmen. That he was so successful in doing so shows that he was a man to be reckoned with.

Joan's mother was a woman of character and independent means. Her means were not all that conspicuous, but the little stone house in which she raised her children was part of her dowry. She also inherited land in the nearby town of Vouthon, where she was born. Her character is best illustrated by the fact that in 1440—and thus long after both Joan and her father had died—she gathered up the strength to move to Orléans and begin rehabilitation proceedings for her daughter. She was one of the plaintiffs at Joan's rehabilitation trial. She claimed to be old and ailing at the time.[6]

Both of Joan's parents were very devout: "good Catholics" was the phrase witnesses used.[7] Her mother's last name seems to be indicative of this latter fact. It has been suggested that Romée is not a last name at all, but an appellative given to pilgrims who went to Rome. Although there is no record of Joan's mother's ever having gone to Rome, it is known that she often went on shorter pilgrimages. She was on a pilgrimage to Puy when Joan first met Charles of Valois at Chinon, and she was on a pilgrimage once again when Charles was crowned in Reims.

Nothing extraordinary is reported about Joan's earliest childhood. She was baptized in the church of Domrémy in an octagonal basin, which can still be seen in the town's little church today, and had many godparents, as was customary in that day and age. In her earliest years, she was taught everything she needed to know in order to care for a household, which did not, of course, include reading or writing, but spinning and sewing. She seems to have taken pride in her ability to sew and spin, or perhaps hers was just exasperation. At her trial, she claimed that there was nothing anyone in Rouen could teach her as far as either was concerned. Catherine le Royer, in whose house Joan stayed when her military adventures were about to begin, claims that her boast was not unfounded.[8] She also herded her father's animals—which were cattle and not sheep—and did some light fieldwork. All of this was quite normal for a girl of her circumstances at the time.

Like all children, Joan liked to play, run in the fields, dance, and sing songs and often did so around the "Fairy Tree" or "Ladies' Tree," a large beech tree which the children of Domrémy were wont to gather around. Like most girls, she picked flowers, wove them into wreaths and garlands. In the

month of May, she would hang these wreaths on the "Ladies
Tree" in order to honor Mary, the Mother of God.[9] She had several choice playmates—Hauviette and Mengette—with whom
she would picnic and play. Like all children from Domrémy, she
was very strongly Armagnac.

Joan was also considered to be a very devout child. She was
often seen going to Church with her mother and other women;
on Saturdays in May she went on pilgrimages to Notre Dame de
Bermont. She would kneel and cross herself whenever she heard
the church bells ring,[10] and she was charitable; she gave alms to
the poor, nursed the sick. Her childhood friend Simonin Musnier
testified that she nursed him back to health when he was seriously ill.[11] Several witnesses at her rehabilitation trial even claim that
they poked fun at her for her childhood devotion.[12]

There is a temptation to do for the very young Joan what both
late Antiquity and the Middle Ages did for the early life of
Christ—that is to rewrite her youth along the lines of what was to
come—and to see in her early devotion the mark of a prophet to
come. There are about as many sentimental revisitations of Joan's
early childhood as there are apocryphal gospels of the childhood
of Christ. Perceval de Boulainvilliers, the contemporary from
whom the date of her birth as been accepted, for instance, claims
that her birth was greeted by a jubilation of the animals in the
vicinity of her home: cocks crowed, donkeys brayed, horses
neighed.[13] Or again, one of the witnesses at her rehabilitation trial
relates that Joan so loved church bells when she was a child that
she was deeply distressed when the hours were not tolled on time,
or at all. She thus went to the bell-toller, Perrin Drappier—who
is the person who related the story—and offered him the best
bribe she could think of—her sweets—to ensure that the *Compline*
and the *Angelus* were regular and timely.[14] While Joan was young
enough when she did take off from Domrémy in 1429 to be considered a precocious prophet (Christ was thirty when he left

Nazareth), there was nothing truly extraordinary about her child-hood devotion given both the time and place in which she lived, and above all, the household in which she grew up.

The Middle Ages were a time of faith. They were an age in which everything was perceived as being somehow related to God and his Church, to the ultimate battle between good and evil, and as being meaningful because of that relation. Time was God's gift. Church bells marked the medieval's day. They sounded in the morning as he woke up; they sounded at noon, when he rested; they sounded in the evening to mark the end of his workday. They sounded when he was baptized, and they sounded when he died. Religious festivities marked his calendar. They issued in the sea-sons; they marked the heart of the seasons; and they marked the end of the seasons. They gave the seasons meaning. Religious locations provided vacation resorts. They were the pilgrimage sites, which restored the body and the soul. Time was God's gift. This is why it made perfect sense for the medieval mind to think that it was wrong to charge interest on a loan. Charging interest meant making a person pay for time, and time was God's gift. No one could charge money for that. And as time was God's gift, so too was everything else: life, the earth, happiness.

In an age such as this, it is not too terribly surprising that the young Joan was devout. She was in this respect no different from most of the people of her day. Her own parents were devout. It was her mother who taught her the basic prayers: the *Pater Noster*, the *Ave Maria*, and the *Credo*. (It is, of course, true that religious par-ents need not necessarily have religious children, and that a reli-gious age is known to beget the worst atheists. The aftermath of Joan's death demonstrates this very point. Gilles de Rais, one of her companions-at-arms, became involved in black magic after she was executed in Rouen and turned into one of the most barbarous serial killers of all times. He was the prototype for Bluebeard.) But devotion itself is not necessarily the sign of an incumbent spiritu-al mission, or the principal cause of it. Joan's own parents were both very devout, but neither of them had extraordinary missions.

The extraordinary took place, or rather started to take place, when Joan was about thirteen. That is when she reported first having heard her voices. She "was in her father's garden," she told the Inquisitor, the first time she heard the voice. "It was on a day in summer at about noon . . . The voice came from the right, from the direction of the church, and was accompanied by a bright light." The voice told Joan about the pitiful state of the kingdom of France and that she must help restore order in it.

Joan was at first terrified, both of the voice, and probably of the task.[15] But the voice returned, two or three times a week. After having thrice heard it, she told Cauchon, she knew that it was an angel's. Shortly thereafter, she added, she discovered that it was the Archangel Michael's. After some time had passed, she continued, she heard other voices: those of Saint Catherine and Saint Margaret.

Joan adamantly refused to give a detailed account of her conversations with the voices at her trials—even though she did inform her accusers that she was more forthcoming with both Charles of Valois and Robert of Baudricourt. She even refused to give an unconditional oath at her Rouen trial, lest she might be forced to reveal more about her visions than she cared—or promised—to share. This was a daily ordeal for Joan. Every time she stood on the witness stand at Rouen, which was at least once a day since she was the only witness at her trial, she was called upon to swear to tell the truth, the whole truth, and nothing but the truth. Every time she was asked to do so, Joan refused to take the oath in its full formula. She pointed out that there were some things that she would not tell her judges, things that she had promised not to tell, and which had no bearing on the trial itself.[16] What she did reveal are two main things: that the voices taught her to be devout—to go to mass often, to pray—and, that they enjoined her to save France.

The voices gave Joan information regarding future events.

Joan knew, for instance, that she was going to be wounded at the battle of Orléans sometime before the battle took place. She mentions the fact in a letter to the dauphin, which was written on April 22, 1429, two weeks before the battle took place. But she also told her confessor the same thing the night before she was wounded. She even added that she would be wounded "above the breast."[17] She also knew that she was going to be captured by the English months before she actually was.

The voices also helped her identify people. Joan recognized both Robert de Baudricourt and Charles of Valois on the spot without ever having seen either of them before the event. She herself claimed that it was her voices that helped her do so.[18] The voices consoled her. Throughout her trial Joan often remarked that she would not have been able to stand the pressure (and perhaps the extreme loneliness) of her Rouen trial had it not been for her voices' consolation. They also gave her great joy. Joan confessed to her judges that she was always a bit anguished when they left her.[18]

It is not clear how many voices Joan heard, or whose exactly they were. Here again it is Joan who refused to give her judges exhaustive information. One must not forget that most of the first hand information from Joan comes from the transcripts of her Rouen trials. And at the Rouen trials, Joan was not in friendly hands. The main three voices were those of the Archangel Michael and the Saints Catherine and Margaret. However, Joan told her accusers in Rouen that the Archangel Michael did not always appear alone. He was often accompanied by a choir of angels. Whether the angelic hosts spoke to her, too, and whether they ever appeared to her without St. Michael is not known. At her trial once again, she let drop the information that the Archangel Gabriel had also appeared to her. At her rehabilitation trial, on the other hand, one of her companions-at-arms related that Joan had told him that Charlemagne and St. Louis had both also appeared to her.[19]

3

From Domrémy to Vaucouleurs

> I am but a poor girl who does not
> know how to ride a horse, or make war.
>
> —*Joan of Arc*

JOAN LIVED A RATHER NORMAL LIFE for several years after she began to hear her voices. She must have continued to do her chores in those years—sewing, spinning, and farming. Such seems to have been her—and her voices'—intent. At her Rouen trial she told her accusers that she did not inform anyone in Domrémy about her visions—not even her parish priest or any other confessor—or about their call for help. Witnesses at her rehabilitation trial report that she did let some "meaningful phrases" about her quest slip from time to time, especially when her stay in Domrémy was coming to an end.[1] They also point out, however, that they did not understand what she had told them until much later, which means, of course, that Joan did not mean for her meaningful phrases to relay the full truth of her quest.

Joan's silence had many causes. Fear was one of these. At her trial, she claimed that she did not inform her parents about the voices—or what they said—for fear that they would not let her embark on her mission. She also claimed that she was afraid that the Burgundians would have tried to stop her if they had heard of her before she actually did leave Domrémy.[2] And since word travels once it is shared, she must have felt it best not to tell any

With her celebrated moral zeal, Joan drives les filles de joie from an army camp. (Courtesy Giraudon/Art Resources, NY)

This image of the Virgin Mary in armor was commissioned for an altarpiece by the Teutonic Knights in Joan's lifetime and later confused with Joan of Arc herself. (Courtesy Erich Lessing/Art Resource, NY)

of her friends about her experiences.

It is also true that she might have feared becoming the target of her friends' jests. Joan was poked fun at for her childhood devotion, as her own friends relate, and she probably surmised that the jeering would increase if she related the content of her new experiences to any one of her friends. Her silence cannot, however, just have been caused by either her caution or the natural desire to avoid being considered the town fool. Had it been, she would have told her confessor about the visions. Confessors, after all, are bound by a vow of silence.

The deeper cause of Joan's silence seems rather to have been her need to come to terms with the fact that she did have extraordinary experiences, and that those extraordinary experiences called for extraordinary deeds on her part. Years later, she let the Inquisitor know just how difficult it was for her to believe in the voices. She said that she "was afraid of her voice" the first time she heard it, and that she had had "grave doubts" regarding its identity.[3] Indeed, she related that she did not believe that the voice she heard was an angel's until she had heard it "three times" and added that she did not know that the angel was the Archangel Michael specifically until she had seen him "many times." She also pointed out that she was well aware of the fact that her belief in her voices was contingent upon her own willingness to believe: "Asked how she recognized that they were angels, she answered that she believed it very soon and had the desire to believe it."[4] And her willingness, as her own testimony points out, was not easily swayed.

Nor was believing in the voices the only problem. Accepting the mission they proposed must have been just as difficult, if not more so. The voices called her to leave home. They were explicit and urgent on the matter. "The voice said to her two or three times a week that she, Joan, must leave and go into France . . . the voice told her that she would go into France, and that she could no longer remain where she was." But as exciting as the prospect must have been to her, leaving home meant leaving her family, the world she knew, and Joan was aware—and wary—of this. She did not tell her parents of her departure for "France" when it eventually did take place, because she was afraid it would hurt them. "The voices were quite content that she should tell them, had it not been for the pain it would have caused them if she told them about her departure; as far as she was concerned, she would not have told them for anything." Nor did she tell Hauviette, who remembered the fact years later.[5]

The voices called Joan to military action and to save France, and Joan was uncertain about both of these things. She confessed to the Inquisitor that once the voices clarified what she was to do she responded that she could not possibly do what they asked of her: She did not know how to ride, she had never borne arms, and she knew nothing about leading armies.

Military action wasn't the only thing that was not settled in Joan's mind. She did not quite know at first what "saving France" meant or what it entailed. Even at her trial, Joan only had a very vague notion of what "France" was, the specific troubles France was facing, or the specific remedies for those troubles. One could not expect a thirteen-year-old from a little border village to be fully informed about such matters. Joan needed time to understand what exactly she was called to do and she used that time wisely. When she finally left Domrémy she had a very clear notion of her goals. She expressed them neatly at her first Inquisition: She had to raise the siege of Orléans, crown the king, liberate the duke of Orléans, and deliver France from the English.

All of this makes Joan's silence perfectly understandable. Joan must have been quite reticent to believe in and divulge news about an improbable encounter which called her to do what, for all intents and purposes, was considered impossible. And she must have silently looked for solitude—someplace where—and time when—she could be alone, both so that she could reflect on the new dimension cut into her being and so that she could communicate with her voices. Joan's voices visited her quite often, and it's hard to imagine that they would have done so—or that she would have wanted them to do so—while she was at the dinner table with her family, or when she was spinning with her mother in front of the fireplace.

This is not to say that Joan became a recluse. There were many witnesses from Domrémy at her rehabilitation trial, and they would certainly have said something about a drastic transformation in Joan if it had indeed taken place. It is to say that some change must have occurred in her habits or perhaps even her demeanor. The Joan in battle and at her trial was an extrovert. The search for solitude that accompanies extraordinary experiences must, therefore, have entailed some alteration in her behavior. Joan herself told the Inquisitor that once she heard her voices she "gave herself to games and frolics" as little as possible. Witnesses at her rehabilitation trial recount that she was wont to disappear during her pasturing duties to go to a nearby chapel to pray.[6]

This must both have been painful for Joan (extroverts need to share their joys and doubts with others) and aroused suspicion in those people who best knew her. Indeed, despite Joan's silence, or possibly because of it, her parents must have guessed something about the change that was taking place in her. It's reported that "her father and mother took great care to guard her and held her in great subjection"—and arranged to have her engaged to be married to a man from Domrémy, whose name is unknown—precisely in the years that separated her first encounter with the angel and her first public appearance as God's chosen warrior.

The direct cause of the strictness, and the engagement, was a prophetic dream of Joan's father. In his dream he saw Joan ride away with an army. "When she was still in the home of her father and mother, it was several times told her by her mother that her father said that he had dreamt that the said Joan his daughter would go away with men-at-arms."

This must have been a horrifying thought for Joan's father. Women who tagged along with armies were those of dubious repute. Joan herself realized this. In her account of the matter she added that her mother informed her that after his dream, her father resolved that he would personally drown his daughter if she were to run off with an army. He even had his two sons swear that they would do it for him.

> Truly, if I thought that thing would happen which I am afraid of where my daughter is concerned, I would want you to drown her, and if you did not do it, then I would drown her myself.[6]

In light of this dream, Joan's parents' planning her betrothal was a logical thing. Marriage was the easiest way for them to avert what they naturally thought was an indecorous future for their daughter.

Whatever the cause of the engagement was, it took place. And what most probably struck Joan's parents as odder than any of the unusual behavior which she must have displayed up to that point was her refusal to abide by their decision. Joan, who was ordinarily an obedient child, did not allow herself to be swayed by her father's wish. She refused to marry. The refusal, she told the Inquisitor, was a direct result of her visions. After having heard her voices, she swore to keep her virginity until she had accomplished what God had asked of her.

Breaking an engagement had legal consequences. Joan therefore was called upon to acquit herself before an ecclesiastical court in Toul. There was nothing extraordinary about this. What was extraordinary is that she defended herself alone—without legal counsel—and, as it turned out, successfully. No further word was mentioned about marriage.

Joan's external life began to change drastically in 1428, when her voices instructed her to go to Vaucouleurs to retain Robert de Baudricourt, the bailiff of the town, as an escort. She was to proceed to Chinon, speak to Charles of Valois, the dauphin, and begin to raise an army. The choice of Baudricourt was a natural one: Vaucouleurs, like Domrémy, was staunchly Armagnac. Unlike

Domrémy, however, it was clearly on the lands of the royal house of France—its bailiff was the dauphin's man. It was also conspicuously larger than Domrémy.

Joan did not tell her parents about her orders. Rather, she asked her parents if she might go to visit her cousin Jeanette, who lived in Burey-le-Petit, a little town which was very close to Vaucouleurs. She had an excellent excuse for a visit. Her cousin was pregnant with her first child at that time and needed help around the house.

Arrangements were quickly made for the visit. Jeanette's husband, Durand Laxart, to whom Joan referred as "Uncle Durand" since he was much older than she, drove to Domrémy, picked her up and brought her to his home. This took place probably sometime in May of 1428.[8]

At her Rouen trial, Joan said that she stayed with her cousin for roughly a week before she revealed the real purpose of her visit to Durand. At that point, as Durand himself confirmed years later, she told him about her voices and mission, and convinced him to take her to Robert de Baudricourt.[9] Convincing Durand was not all that difficult. All Joan had to do, it seems, was point out that her mission had been prophesied. It had been foretold that "as France had been lost by a woman, it would be restored by a virgin."

The prophecy was one of many that traveled by way of mouth throughout France in those days. Its origin is a matter of some contention. At the time, many people held that its origin was King Arthur's Merlin. Merlin was held in more or less the same esteem by late medieval popular belief as Nostradamus was in the years to come. However, another medieval visionary had prophesied something similar. At Joan's examination at Poitiers, Jean Erault, one of the members of the commission which examined her, recalled that Marie d'Avignon, a well-known visionary of the late fourteenth century, had had a vision in which she saw weapons and was afraid that it was she who would have to bear them. But she was told that they would be borne by a virgin who would come after her.[10]

What is more interesting than the prophecy is that Durand Laxart paid it heed. Family relations tend not to view their kin—especially their in-laws—as extraordinary. *Nemo propheta in patria*—no one is a prophet in his own country. As such, it is a great tribute to Durand that he did believe Joan and agree to accompany her to the bailiff of Vaucouleurs.

Joan had an audience with Robert de Baudricourt immediately. That was, however, the only positive note of the day. She informed Baudricourt that she was sent by God to aid the Armagnac cause, and that he should send a missive to Charles of Valois, the dauphin, and warn him to stand ready for battle but not to engage in it directly. For any warlike efforts on the dauphin's part would have a disastrous outcome at that time. She added that Baudricourt should tell the dauphin not to despair. For God, who was the true Lord of France, had decided to grant him the kingdom of France, and would send him substantial help by the middle of the following Lent. She herself would be the one who would see to it that he was crowned.[11]

Baudricourt simply laughed at Joan's message. He had certainly witnessed something extraordinary. A seventeen-year-old girl in a "red dress," who had none of the prerequisites of a medieval war chief, had just promised to do what no Armagnac even dreamt was possible at that time. Fortunately, he was in a good mood. After having threatened to hand her over to his soldiers,[12] he simply sent Joan home with the recommendation that some sense be beaten into her head. Durand relates that Joan's response to Baudricourt was to turn to her "uncle," give him his cloak, and walk out.[13]

Joan returned to Domrémy none too disheartened by her lack of success. The fact that there is no significant information about her return seems to indicate that her Vaucouleurian interlude did not have any real effects, at least as far as her relations with her parents were concerned, and that her parents had heard nothing about her visit to Baudricourt. Then again, the months following her first public appearance as God's chosen warrior were not easy ones.

In the late spring of 1428, the Anglo-Burgundians decided that the time had come for them to put an end to Armagnac dissension in northeastern France. They launched a substantial offensive against Vaucouleurs and the towns surrounding it. Vaucouleurs was attacked in June; Domrémy in July. It was in that very July that Joan, her family, their cattle, and what seems to have been most of the population of Domrémy escaped to Neufchâteau where they stayed for a fortnight waiting for things to calm down at home.

During that fortnight they stayed at the inn of a woman named La Rousse (the redhead). Joan, who loathed inactivity, spent her time in Neufchâteau helping her hostess around the inn. She and Hauviette, her best friend, washed dishes and cooked. Joan even brought the local cattle out to pasture (perhaps more out of her need for solitude than her need to do something). It is also possible that Joan did not spend the entire fortnight at Neufchâteau. She seems to have been called upon to defend herself at the ecclesiastical court at Toul for having broken her engagement right around the time when she and her family were at Neufchâteau.

There are no records about the months following the Burgundian raid. But they were probably busy ones. The town had rebuilding and restocking to take care of, and very little time in which to do so. Winter was only three months away. Joan returned to Vaucouleurs in January. She left Domrémy secretly, it seems, and in haste. She did not even say good-bye to her closest friend.

Joan's second stay in Vaucouleurs was very different from her first. It lasted six weeks. Joan spent most of those weeks in Vaucouleurs, not in Burey with her "Uncle" Durand. She stayed at the home of Catherine and Henri Le Royer, who lived in the town itself. She saw Baudricourt twice during that stay. Nothing came of her first visit. The bailiff of Vaucouleurs simply sent Joan away.

The air had changed, however. News of Joan had begun to spread among both the townspeople of Vaucouleurs and the local nobility. Joan's own hostess, Catherine Le Royer, had become one of her allies. Another was a minor nobleman, Jean de Metz, who claims to have given her the wherewithal to clothe her for the military life she was to lead. Metz, who was part of the garrison at Vaucouleurs, swore fealty to Joan after she had confided to him just how urgent it was for her to speak to Baudricourt. He gave a vivid account of the event:

> I said to her: "*M'amie*, what are you doing here? Must the king be chased out of his kingdom, and we be English?" To which she replied: "I have come here, to this royal town, to speak to the Sire de Baudricourt, so that he may take me, or have me taken, to the dauphin. But he pays no attention to me or to my words. But I must be with the dauphin before mid-Lent, though I wear my legs to the knees; for no one in the world . . . can recover the kingdom of France. There is no help but me, though I should prefer to spin beside my poor mother . . . But I must go, and I will do it because my Lord wishes me to do it." I asked her who her Lord was, and she answered: "It is God." I then gave Joan my sworn word, taking her by the hand, that with God's help I would take her to the king."[14]

What is more significant by far is that Charles II, the duke of Lorraine, had Joan sent for after Baudricourt had "repulsed" her for the second time.

Joan went to Nancy, which was some twenty-five miles east of Vaucouleurs, prepared to convert the duke to her cause. She asked him for a body of men-at-arms to accompany her to Charles of Valois. The duke, who was a Burgundian, paid that request little attention. He had summoned her for very private reasons. His, it seems, was not the best of health and he wanted

Joan to cure him. She told him to put his mistress aside rather than bother her. The duke must have been extremely impressed with—or perhaps even frightened—by Joan. He gave her four francs and a black horse for her pains.[15]

In the meanwhile, the townspeople of Vaucouleurs wanted to make up for Baudricourt's disbelief. For weeks they had witnessed what must have been an intense silent fray between the incandescent Joan and the staunch Baudricourt. Joan went to Our Lady of the Vaults, the chapel in the town's castle, every morning to pray.[16] Baudricourt, on the other hand, sat in the castle every day, busying himself with other matters and probably hoping that something would arise that might sway his mind with regards to the Joan matter. When Joan returned from Nancy, the townspeople took matters into their own hands. They bought Joan another horse, gave her another set of men's clothing, which they had made especially for her—"hose, leggings, and everything necessary"—and stood ready to personally accompany her to the dauphin.

This must have been tempting to Joan, who was anxious to go. Catherine Le Royer's comparison is telling on this point. She claims that "Joan wanted [to go] so much, and the time was as heavy to her as if she were a pregnant woman, until she could be taken to the dauphin."[17] Joan started out on her journey to the dauphin in the company of Durand Laxart and a man named Jacques Alain, who quite likely represented the town as a whole, since the entire town was involved in paying for Joan's accouterment. Something, however, told Joan to stop and backtrack to Vaucouleurs. For once the party reached Saint-Nicholas-de-Septfonds, Joan stopped, entered the local chapel, and prayed. When she emerged, she told her comrades that they had all better return home, because she was not meant to leave in that way.[18]

Upon her return to Vaucouleurs, Baudricourt finally responded to Joan's plea. He called upon her at the Le Royers', accompanied by Jean Fournier, the parish priest of Vaucouleurs, whom the bailiff had asked to exorcise any evil spirits that may have hovered around the household. Joan, who must have been used to many different sorts of warding by then, responded by kneeling in front of the priest. (She later let Catherine Le Royer know that the priest had done ill by reciting the exorcism, since he had heard her confession, and knew better than to think evil of her.[19]) It's not known how the priest replied. Baudricourt, on the other hand, proceeded to reimburse the townspeople for the weapons and horse they had given Joan, and agreed to give her a bodyguard for her visit to the dauphin. At her Rouen trial, she recalled that he then gave her a sword and told her, "Go, and let come what may."

How Joan managed to convince Baudricourt to give her an escort will always be a mystery. At her trial she claimed that she had given him some sign which demonstrated the divine origin of her mission, although she did not specify what that sign was, or might have been, or why it took him so long to believe in it.

Legends and scholars, on the other hand, have offered a myriad of other possible explanations. Legend claims that Joan told Baudricourt that a battle was about to be lost in the vicinity of Orléans, and that he received a missive sometime thereafter that confirmed her claim. The battle in question was the disastrous "battle of the Herrings."[20] It took place the day before Joan left, and was one of the most humiliating losses suffered by the French. The commanders of the garrison of the besieged city of Orléans attempted to raise their morale by attacking a convoy of fifteen hundred men, led by Sir John Fastolf, which was bringing the English besiegers a fresh store of victuals, which were salted herrings and other "lenten stuff." Their plans quickly went awry. They had miscalculated the size of the English convoy, and were routed.

Baudricourt's assent may, on the other hand, have simply been ordered by the dauphin. The bailiff had, after all, written his liege lord about Joan, asking what he should do, and it is known that a royal courier, Colet de Vienne, was in Vaucouleurs in those days. He was a member of the entourage that eventually left for Chinon with Joan. Some claim that it was public opinion that swayed Baudricourt. This is possible. Then again, the cause may have been the escalation in the Anglo-Burgundian offensive, for the attacks on Vaucouleurs and Domrémy were just a part of a larger venture whose aim was to conquer the heart of the lands loyal to Charles of Valois. The Armagnacs, who had not won a major battle in many years, needed a miracle at that point. Whatever the cause was, the impossible had begun to take place. An illiterate peasant girl set out to break all of the rules of medieval warfare.

Saint Joan of Arc, from *Le Champion de Dames* by Martin le Franc (15th c.), resembles a dashing cavalier. In *Les Champion*, Joan was compared to Judith, who killed the tyrant Holofernes to save her people. (Courtesy Giraudon/Art Resource, NY)

IN ICONEM IANAE VOGOLAVRIAE VIRAGINIS AVRELIAE ·
VIRGO REDIT · GALLO MVTA VEL IMAGINE FOELIX ·
QVAM NVMEN QVONDAM PATRIAE NON MACHINA MISIT
SVBSIDIO · AVGVRIVM BONE REX HENRICE SALVTA ·
DE COELIS EXCITA TVIS VIRGO ALTERA VOTIS ·
· FORTVNET REGNI AVSPICIVM · LANCEMQZ RETRACTET
VTRAQZ VT ANTIQVVM TVA SAECLA RECVDAT IN AVRVM
G·V·G·PP·1581·

**A portrait commissioned by the aldermen of Orléans ignores the
male dress that Joan historically wore.** (Courtesy Giraudon/Art
Resource, NY)

4

Chinon

Gentil dauphin, I am come and sent by God
to bring aid to you and your kingdom.

—Joan of Arc

JOAN LEFT VAUCOULEURS FOR CHINON, the dauphin's residence,
no more taken aback by her success with Baudricourt than she had
been by her initial failure, and as sure of getting to Chinon as she
had been of getting through to the bailiff. Witnesses report that
she responded to their warnings regarding the dangers of the trip
by telling them that "the path was open to her, and if there were
soldiers on the way, she had God, her Lord, who would clear the
road for her to go to the dauphin . . . For she was born for this."[1]

It was February 12, 1429.[2] By that time, Joan had had her
hair cut, doffed her red dress and donned men's clothing. Robert
de Baudricourt had given her a sword and she had an escort of six:
Jean de Metz, Bertrand de Poulegny, the latter's two servants, a
soldier named Richard, and a royal messenger, Colet de Vienne.

Joan's lack of fear to the contrary, their journey was a dangerous one. In order to reach Chinon she and her party had to travel
through lands which were solidly in Anglo-Burgundian hands.
Therefore, they mostly traveled by night, and avoided most of the
towns. This, too, was dangerous. At the time the French countryside was full of robber bands—and unpaid soldiers—waiting for
small parties to ambush. Nor was it a particularly clement time to

travel. France had just had a bout of heavy rains—rivers threatened to overflow, fields were flooded, and the roads were very muddy. And the moon, which was their one source of light for their night travel, was waning.[3] The party nonetheless made it through unscathed and quickly. Despite the treacherous conditions, the company traveled three-hundred-odd miles from Vaucouleurs to Chinon, fording no fewer than six rivers, in eleven days.

Not all of those eleven days were spent on the road. Nor were all of them spent in the wilderness. The party spent at least one night in a monastery, when they approached St. Urbain. They also entered the town of Auxerre, where Joan attended mass.[4] This was probably a bit foolhardy. Auxerre was a staunchly Burgundian town at that time, and a party of travelers, albeit a small one, was a conspicuous thing in those days of harsh weather. Years after the event took place people from Auxerre still remembered having seen a small company of travelers, which included a very young sixteen-year-old peasant from Lorraine, passing through the town in those days.[5] But Joan insisted on attending mass. She had not had the chance to do so during the journey, as Bertrand de Poulegny was later to point out.

The party's longest stay, however, was in Fierbois, which was a rather well known pilgrimage site situated just some fifteen miles from Chinon, where they stopped on the eighth day in order to inform the dauphin of Joan's arrival. They waited two full days for his response. Joan spent those days in prayer. Fierbois was the ideal place, it seems, for her to do so. Its chapel was dedicated to St. Catherine (her St. Catherine), and legend had it that Charles Martel, Charlemagne's grandfather, had left his sword there. The stay in Fierbois also gave Joan the chance to attend mass. At Rouen she was later to recall that she attended three masses in one day while she was in Fierbois.

The party left Fierbois for Chinon on the morning of the twenty-third of February immediately after having had word from the dauphin. Chinon was a magnificent castle. Its walls encompassed the top of the high ridge overlooking the town of Chinon, and there were three separate fortresses within those walls: the castle of St. George, the middle castle, and the castle of Coudray. It was virtually impregnable. Since its external walls encompassed the top of the ridge, there was a sheer drop outside of them, which meant that they could not be scaled.

Chinon was Charles's favorite residence. Ironically, it was also one of the favorite residences of the Plantagenet kings of England while it was still in their hands. Henry II of England, the founder of the dynasty, built Chinon's castle of St. George, and died there in 1189. Such was the symbolic value of Chinon that King Philip Augustus of France lay siege on it for almost an entire year in his assault on English dominion over France. As such, it is one of those wonderful jests of fortune that the first encounter between the uncrowned king of France and the soon-to-be liberator of France from the English took place there. The assault on English dominion of France was to begin in an English-built castle.

The details of that first encounter are a bit obscure. At her Rouen trial Joan claimed that she arrived at Chinon at noon and went straight to find lodgings. After having lunched, she continued, she went to the king and was immediately given an audience. From her testimony one gathers that she had no trouble at all obtaining one. She explicitly stated that she reached her king without having to overcome any obstacles.[6]

This hardly seems likely. Although it is certain that the king had heard of Joan (news of her trip to Chinon had spread throughout France by that time, and the dauphin's own cousin, Jean d'Alençon, had cut short a hunting trip to make for the dauphin's castle with the explicit intent of meeting Joan), there were multitudes of visionaries, who claimed to be able to do all manner of extraordinary things. And these visionaries regularly beat at the doors of powerful people to be given a chance to do so. It would seem logical for royalty, even those royals in danger of losing their kingdoms, to have some sort of screening process to protect themselves.

That Charles had an active screen is corroborated by witnesses of Joan's arrival, who claimed that Joan was made to wait a few days before seeing the dauphin. Joan was questioned by the dauphin's council regarding her intent. She was very impatient with the council, and refused to give them detailed information about herself, or her message for the dauphin.

> She began by saying that she would say nothing, except directly to the king. But it was put to her that it was in the king's name that she was being asked to explain the motive for her mission. 'I have,' she said, 'two things as a mandate from the King of Heaven—one to raise the siege of Orléans; the other to take the king to Reims for his anointing and coronation. [7]

Whether Joan, as she herself claimed, was immediately admitted to the dauphin's chamber or not, she did have an audience with him and fulfilled her promise of recognizing him on the spot. Joan had made this promise, or boast as some prefer to see it, in the letter she sent the dauphin from Fierbois.

The encounter between Joan and the dauphin is one of the most embellished events in Joan's life. At her Rouen trial, Joan claimed that the hall in which she met the dauphin was filled with "three hundred knights" and that it was blazing with the light from "some fifty torches, not to mention the spiritual light."[8] This is not surprising. Joan had already begun to create a stir. There were many people like d'Alençon, who were eager to see Joan face to face.

Joan was led through the crowd by Louis de Bourbon. Charles, on the other hand, had decided to put Joan to the test. He dressed in rather simple clothes and had one of his courtiers dress in royal ones in hopes of fooling her. It is also said that Charles stood to the side of the hall, trying to make himself as inconspicuous as possible to Joan. Joan was, however, not deceived by the clothes or Charles's attempt to hide. She walked

straight up to Charles, knelt before him, and said, "gentil
dauphin, I am come and am sent by God to bring aid to you and
your kingdom."[8] To which Charles responded that she was mis-
taken. He was not the dauphin. The dauphin, he claimed, was
another man, and pointed to one of his elaborately dressed
courtiers. Joan was not fooled. She responded to Charles, "In
God's name, *gentil dauphin*, it is you and none other."[10]

Joan and the dauphin went out of earshot and had a very private
conversation in which she gave him some proof of the divine origin
of her mission.[11] Joan herself told the Inquisitor that she had done
so. Witnesses corroborate her claim. They mention that the
dauphin was radiant after his conversation with Joan; others add
that the dauphin "appeared to have seen the Holy Ghost Himself"
after his conversation with Joan.[12] The most convincing evidence of
the fact that Charles was struck by what Joan told him in their secret
conversation is that he had royal quarters put at her disposition
immediately thereafter. Joan moved into the tower of Coudray,
which was in the west wing of the castle at Chinon. Charles also
assigned Joan a page, Louis de Coutes, and a squire, Jean d'Aulon.

Charles's choice of quarters is rather ominous. In the fourteenth
century, King Philip IV, who was called Phillip the Fair, used the
tower of Coudray to imprison the last grand master of the Knights
Templar, when he decided to put an end to that order. For some,
Joan's being housed in the tower of Coudray is a portent of her own
tragic end, and of the treachery of the kings of France. Most probably Charles's choice was simply very practical. The tower of Coudray
was very close to the royal quarters—a little bridge connected them.

The matter of the proof Joan gave Charles of the divine origin of her mission has been the subject of debate ever since Joan
gave it. Joan's Inquisitor and his tribunal were certainly anxious
to determine what the nature of that proof was. They questioned
her on the point with a ferocity, which was unusual even for
them. Scholars, too, have hotly debated the point. Some claim
that Joan gave the dauphin some proof of the fact that he was not

Equestrian Statue of Joan of Arc.
(Courtesy Foto Marburg/Art Resource, NY)

Above: **Jean of Arc lead before Charles VII.** (Courtesy
Giraudon/Art Resource, NY)

Below: **Tapestry, German (15th c.). Joan of Arc Entering Chinon.**
(Courtesy Snark/Art Resource, NY)

a bastard, as his own mother had led people to believe after he had had John the Fearless killed. Others believe that Joan repeated the exact content of one of the dauphin's silent prayers to God (although they do not concur on the content of that prayer).[13] Others yet claim that the "bastardy theory" is pure invention and therefore that the secret could not have involved it.[14]

Whatever the proof was, what is certain is that it did not persuade Charles for very long. Following their encounter, he had Joan examined by those theologians who were present at Chinon. It was a formal hearing in which she was questioned on matters regarding the nature of her faith and mission.[15] The hearing appears to have gone well for Joan. Its verdict did not, however, convince the dauphin. He had Joan sent to Poitiers two days afterward, so that she might be examined by those masters of theology of the University of Paris, who had fled there after their city had fallen into Burgundian hands.

Charles's reticence, his need for official ecclesiastical approval of Joan, was not unreasonable. Joan's quest, her claim to have been sent by God to wage war against the English, was a controversial one even for the medieval mind. Unlike the modern mind, the medieval mind did not view Joan's claim to have been sent by God to wage war as contradictory per se. War could be a holy thing to the medievals. That is why many medieval kings went on crusades. What made Joan's claim startling to the medieval mind was the thought that one could consider a war among Christians, who were loyal to the pope, a holy war. That did not fit the medieval worldview. In the Middle Ages, Christendom was in some sense perceived as a single body—the mystical body of Christ. Although everyone knew that there were internal wars, such as wars between the members of the single body of Christians, they did not and could not consider those wars holy. The thought that they were holy would have implied that God wanted the different parts of his son's own mystical body to fight among themselves, and that simply did not make sense. What Joan proposed, as such, was per-

ceived as novel and perhaps even scandalous. With his weak position, Charles simply could not risk sending this possible heretic to
war without official Church approval. Doing so would have been
political suicide as well as a possible spiritual suicide.

Joan spent some three weeks in Poitiers, where she was questioned by a large tribunal which included some high-ranking
members of the Church—two bishops, the archbishop of Reims,
and the confessors of the king and queen of France. This was an
official Inquisition. Joan was naturally none too happy for the
loss of time.[16] She was very urgent about getting on with her
business, but no doubt she understood the importance of official
ecclesiastical approval of her mission. She was a lively witness
during her interrogations but not a hostile one.

The exact content of her Poitiers trial is not known. It is her
one trial whose minutes have been lost. This is a great pity. For
not only would an exact account of the Poitiers proceedings have
given a first-hand portrait of Joan which was not tainted by the
animosity of its redactors, it would also have filled in many
blanks. Joan often referred the Rouen commission to the Poitiers
minutes for exact answers to vital questions that they asked her.
What is known about the trial is its verdict, how Joan was examined, a few of her more brash comments, and her prophecies.

The verdict was in Joan's favor. The Inquisition declared that
Joan was indeed a virgin, as she claimed to be. It declared that she
was a good, humble and pious Catholic who had been given a
divine mission, which allowed her to disregard Deuteronomy's
commandment regarding cross-dressing, and to lead the dauphin's
armies in their attempt to raise the siege of Orléans. The verdict
was based upon both Joan's responses to extensive questioning on
the part of the tribunal, some of whom were prominent theologians, and a physical examination which was conducted by Jeanne
de Prouilly and the Lady of Trèves, both of whom were ladies in
waiting to the dauphin's mother-in-law, Yolande of Aragon.

Joan's brashness was such that she branded a vivid memory of herself in the minds of everyone who saw her. Séguin Séguin, the only member of the Poitiers commission who lived long enough to testify at her rehabilitation trial, remembered that she responded to the questions the tribunal posed "with great style." What he seems to have meant by that was not only that her answers were very keen—if not to say astounding, which is what other eyewitnesses claimed—but also that she was very bold and amusing. He remembered Joan's response to the crucial matter regarding the sanctity of the war Joan claimed to have been sent to fight. The commission pointed out that war may not have been the means God had in mind to save France:

> According to what you say, the voice told you that God wishes to deliver the people of France from the calamity in which it finds itself. But if God wishes to deliver the people of France, it is not necessary to have soldiers.[17]

Joan simply responded: "In God's name the soldiers will fight, and God will give the victory."[18] A good-humored man himself, Séguin even tells us that she poked fun at him for his unruly French.

What most struck Séguin, however, were Joan's prophecies. He recalled that Joan had foretold that the dauphin's troops would lift the siege at Orléans; that she would have the dauphin crowned at Rheims; that the English would be vanquished; and that Charles of Orléans, who was being held hostage in England at the time, would return home safely. And, Séguin added, "I have seen all of these things come to pass."[19]

The most important outcome of the Poitiers trial was that it convinced Charles of Valois to place his trust in Joan. This is not to say that he did not need ulterior confirmation of the verdict. He also consulted Jean Gerson, the once-chancellor of both Notre-Dame and the University of Paris, and Jacques Gelu, the archbishop of Embrun, on the matter of Joan. Both advised him to give her a chance. Charles also tried to get papal blessing on the Joan affair.[20]

It was April, 1429. The dauphin nominated Joan *chef de guerre*, ordered a suit of armor to be prepared for her, assigned her two heralds—Ambleville and Guyenne—began to levy some troops, and had some food sent to Orléans. Joan, too, was preparing for battle. While she was still in Poitiers she dictated a letter to the English commanders of the garrisons stationed at Orléans, informing them of her arrival and their imminent defeat. She had one of the clerks at the trial, Jean Erault, write up the letter on March 22, and thus before the verdict was final.

Once the Poitiers verdict was announced on March 24, Joan briefly returned to Chinon, received her commission, and moved on to Tours, where she was measured for the armor the dauphin had ordered for her. While she was there, she also had three standards prepared. One was her own personal standard, which Joan described quite minutely at her Rouen trial. It was made of white linen—boucassin—and depicted Jesus seated on a throne, holding the world in his hand, and with a kneeling angel on either side. The words *Jhesus Maria* were sewn on the sides of the standard. The background was decorated with lilies. The second standard, which was for her company, seems to have depicted the Annunciation. The third standard was to be for the priests who accompanied the army. It bore the Crucifixion.

Joan also found a chaplain for her company—Jean Pasquerel. Both Joan's mother and part of the company, which had escorted Joan to Chinon, had met Pasquerel while they were on a pilgrimage to Puy. Both parties were immediately struck by the priest. But it was the latter who insisted that he come with them to meet Joan. Once Pasquerel and Joan met, they did not separate until Joan was captured at Compiègne. Pasquerel tells of their encounter:

> Those who had brought me spoke, saying, "Joan, we have brought you this good Father; when you to know him well, you will love him much." Joan replied that she was well

Jhesus Maria

[Letter to the English commanders at Orléans]

King of England, and you, duke of Bedford, who call yourself regent of the kingdom of France; you William de la Pole, earl of Suffolk; John, lord Talbot, lord Scales, who call yourselves lieutenants of the said Duke of Bedford, do right in the King of Heaven's sight, and surrender to the Maid, who is here sent by God, the King of Heaven, the keys of all the good towns you have here taken and laid to waste in France. She is come here by God's will to reestablish the Blood Royal, ready to make peace if you will acknowledge her to be right by leaving France and paying for what you have held. And you, archers, companions of war, men-at-arms and others who are before the town of Orléans, return in God's name to your own country. If you do not do so, expect to hear news of the Maid who will come to see you shortly, to your great injury.

King of England, if you do not do thus, know that I am *chef de guerre*, and in whatever place I meet your people in France, I will make them quit it, will they or nil they. And if they will not obey, I will have them all slain. I am sent here by God, the King of Heaven, to drive you, body by body out of the whole of France. And if they do obey, I will be merciful to them.

And do not think otherwise, for you will not gain the Kingdom of France from God, the King of Heaven, son of Saint Mary, as King Charles, the true heir, will; for God, the King of Heaven, wishes it so, and has revealed it through the Maid, who will enter into Paris with a good company. If you will not believe the news sent to you by God and the Maid, we will strike into whatever place we find you and make such great *hay-hay* that none so great has been in France for a thousand years if you will not yield to right. And believe firmly that the King of Heaven will send more strength to the Maid that you will be able to bring up with all your assaults, against her and her good men-at-arms; and on every horizon it will be seen who has the better right from the King of Heaven.

You, duke of Bedford, the Maid begs and requires of you that you discontinue the destruction. If you grant her right, you may still come into her company where the French shall do the greatest feat of arms that was ever done for Christianity. And make answer if you wish to make peace in the city of Orléans; and if you do not do so, may you be reminded of it by your great injuries.

Written this Tuesday of Holy week.[21]

pleased that she had already heard of me, and that on the next day she would like to confess to me. The next day I heard her confession and sang mass before her. From that hour I followed her always and remained with her until Compiègne, where she was captured.[22]

What most astounded Joan's entourage about her preparations was her request for a sword with "five crosses" which, she claimed, was buried behind the altar of the chapel of St. Catherine at Fierbois. Word and a blacksmith were sent to find it. It was precisely where Joan claimed that it would be. It was removed and polished—its rust fell away easily—and delivered to Joan with an array of scabbards—one made of gold cloth, one made of red velvet, and a leather one, which she herself had requested.[23]

In the meanwhile, troops gathered at Blois under the command of Jean d'Alençon, whom the dauphin had commissioned to organize and provision them. Once Joan had completed her own preparations, she set out to meet them. It was April 21. When Joan met her troops she immediately began to work with them, training and tilting. Her mastery in the martial arts was naturally a great source of wonder among her soldiers. Military skills take time and practice to master, time and practice which Joan simply had not had. Jean d'Alençon, who had seen her tilt on the field at Chinon, was so taken aback by her style that he gave her yet another horse—a charger.[24]

What was more important to Joan, however, was the troops' spiritual state. She urged her men to pray, to go to mass, and to take the sacraments—to confess. God did not want the French to lose, she claimed, but he also could not give them victory if they were in a sorry state of soul. She forbade blasphemy, even forcing the officers to clean their language. She chased the female attachments from the camps at sword point. On April 27, 1429, Joan left for Orléans with four thousand men and a host of commanders. They set out singing *Veni Creator*.

The "Bastard of Orléans," later count of Dunois,
fought with Joan in the attack on Paris in 1429.
(Courtesy Giraudon/Art Resource, NY)

5

Orléans

Go, daughter of God, go. I am with you.
—*Joan of Arc*

ORLÉANS HAD BEEN UNDER SIEGE for seven months. Eleven Anglo-Burgundian encampments surrounded the town. Five of them—La Croix Boisée, Fort Londres, Fort Rouen, Fort Paris, and the Bastille de Fleury—fanned out on the northern bank of the Loire, blocking the main five northwestern roads that led to the town. Four more forts—St. Jean le Blanc, the Augustins, the Tourelles, and St. Privéivé–were on the southern bank of the Loire, blocking the three southern roads to Orléans. One of them was on the Île Charlemagne in the Loire itself, blocking river traffic arriving to the town from the west. The last one, the Fort Saint Loup, was to the east of the town.

Despite the impressive array, Orléans was in no immediate danger of capitulating. The town was not completely surrounded by Anglo-Burgundian troops. It still controlled its northeastern gate—the gate of Bourgogne—and the roads that led to it were in Franco-Armagnac hands. This meant that the town could receive fresh supplies. It had received a rather sizable fresh supply of pigs two days before Joan's arrival.[1] It was also armed.

However, this is not to say that the citizens of Orléans were not worried or that their situation was not in the least bit precar-

69

ious. Food did arrive, that is true. And yet the pressure of being under siege—of the constant skirmishes and bombardments—led them to ply the duke of Burgundy with a request for help.[2] It was the English commanders of the siege who kept that request from being met, despite their alliance with the duke. They did not want to be in the unfortunate position of having done all the work and having their idle ally reap all of the benefits.[3]

When Joan and her troops arrived on the evening of April 29 they were a welcome sight. Joan entered the town with the count of Dunois, known as the "Bastard of Orléans," who was the commander of the Franco-Armagnac troops at Orléans. She rode into the town in full armor on a white horse, carrying her standard. An enormous crowd gathered in the streets to greet her. Everyone wanted to touch "her or the horse she rode." And it is reported that everyone who did so felt immediate surcease from the pressure of the siege. "They felt already comforted, as though freed of the siege by the divine virtue that they were told resided in that simple Maid."[4] Such was the crowds' desire to touch Joan, that one of the town's torchbearers set her standard on fire. Joan simply "stuck spurs in her horse, and turned him thus gently towards the pennon, and extinguished the fire as if she had long served in the wars."[5] The crowd clamored at the show of equestrian excellence.

Joan was not quite as happy as the inhabitants of Orléans. When her army left Blois it did not march along the northern bank of the Loire on the road that traveled to Orléans from Blois. It took a long detour to avoid the Anglo-Burgundian troops garrisoned around Orléans. It crossed over to the southern bank of the Loire and marched through the Sologne countryside in the direction of Chécy, which is to the east of Orléans itself. Once it had skirted around the English forts, it crossed the Loire and marched towards Orléans's eastern gate: the gate of Bourgogne. This told Joan that they were not going to attack the English immediately. (It also indicates that she had not planned the route.) This infuriated Joan, who was clearly eager to get on with her mission.

Dunois recounts that he bore the brunt of her impatience. Before their entrance in the city, Joan asked him if he were responsible for the choice of routes. Having been told that he was, but upon the advice of men of great experience, she calmly explained to him that the matter of his counselors' experience was of no concern to her as it should not be to him. For the help she was bringing outstripped human wisdom, and her counsel informed her that the only people whom his caution had helped were the English:

In God's name, the counsel of the Lord God is wiser and surer than yours. You thought you had deceived me, but it is you who have deceived yourselves. For I am bringing you better help than you ever got from any soldier or any city. It is the help of the King of Heaven. It does not come through love of me, but from God himself who, on the petition of Saint Louis and Saint Charlemagne, has had pity on the town of Orléans, and has refused to suffer the enemy to have both the body of the lord of Orléans and his city.[6]

What kept Dunois from responding in tone was a tactical emergency. The army had brought with it the food and equipment necessary to raise the siege at Orléans. These were loaded on sixty carts and some four-hundred-odd beasts of burden, which the commanders intended to send to Orléans by barge once they had skirted around the Anglo-Burgundians. The problem was that doing so was not as easy as they had thought it would be. When they reached the Loire, the heavy contrary winds and the low river did not let them carry out their plans. The Franco-Armagnac relieving force was thus stuck in a vulnerable position. Burdened as it was, it was open to attack. And it could neither proceed toward Orléans without the equipment and victuals (the English would have grabbed them) nor proceed with them.

Entry of Joan into Orléans. (Courtesy Giraudon/Art Resource, NY)

Right: **Joan of Arc Before Orléans.** (Courtesy Giraudon/Art Resource, NY)

Below: **La Pucelle, as Joan was to become known, leads her army.** (Courtesy Erich Lessing/Art Resource, NY)

It was at that point that Joan proved her point to Dunois. As she was reprimanding him, telling him that she was bringing help from the "King of Heaven," "Immediately, at that very moment, the wind, which had been adverse and had absolutely prevented the ships carrying the provisions for the city of Orléans from putting out, changed and became favorable."[7] Dunois believed this to be a miracle and became a firm believer in the *Pucelle*, as he called Joan.

Firm believer or not, he did not heed Joan's request to attack the English immediately. On the morning of the day after Joan had arrived in Orléans, a Franco-Armagnac council of war met to discuss strategy and decided that no action would be taken against the English until reinforcements arrived. Joan left the meeting enraged, and with good reason. The Franco-Armagnac troops stationed at Orléans at that point outnumbered the English ones. Joan's four thousand men were not the only ones at Orléans. Historians estimate that Orléans had housed some four thousand troops of its own before she arrived. English garrisons, on the other hand, were about five thousand men strong at that time.[8] There was, as such, no real need to wait for reinforcements.

What held the Armagnacs back, it seems, were fear and the habit of losing. These, Joan was quickly to realize, were her principal foes. The fight for Orléans was firstly and foremostly a fight against fear. The Armagnac commanders were so accustomed to losing by the time Joan appeared that they dared not tempt fate by going to battle, especially after they had won one. As a result, Joan had to coax, push, and even force them onto the battlefield. It was a daily endeavor.

Joan made the best of her enforced quiet; she had no alternative for the next three days. Reinforcements did not arrive until May 4. Dunois himself had gone to get them, and etiquette demanded that she wait for his return to engage in action. Dunois was the commander of the Armagnac troops in Orléans, after all. So Joan sent her two heralds, Ambleville and Guyenne, with another letter of warning for the English command garrisoned at Fort Saint-Laurent. She approached the other English camps herself in an attempt to parley with them. Since the English refused to parley, she settled on sallying verbally with some Burgundian soldiers quartered in the forts closest to the city. She closely surveyed both the territory surrounding Orléans and the English forts in the company of many of the citizens of the town itself, who were so enthralled with her that they were willing to venture forth from the protection of their town walls unarmed.[9] Joan also spent a lot of time with her troops in Orléans, exhorting them to prepare spiritually for the battle. Above all, she went to mass and prayed.[10]

On the day reinforcements arrived, Dunois informed Joan that the English were also expecting reinforcements and provisions: Fastolf and a fresh force had already reached Janville and were thus only twenty or so miles away. He expected Joan to agree to call for more reinforcements before engaging the enemy. But Joan was, he claims, overjoyed at the news, and ordered him to inform her when the English reinforcements were in sight, on pains of "losing his head."[11]

Joan was evidently aware of the fact that something was about to happen. She did not expect it to come as soon as it did, however. For she went to rest shortly after Dunois had left her, only to wake up with a start and the knowledge that "French blood was flowing." She called her page, scolded him for not having informed her that the battle had begun, called for her armor and standard and made off for the site, not having missed much.

The battle was more of a skirmish than anything else, and was planned by Dunois. What was being fought for was the fort of St. Loup, which was the most isolated of the English encampments. It lay to the east of Orléans itself, and was built on the ruins of an old abandoned monastery. When Joan arrived at the scene, it is claimed, a roar went up among the French troops, who redoubled their efforts and won the day with ease. They killed one hundred forty-four English, took roughly forty prisoners, and completely demolished the fort. Joan's reaction to the victory was mixed. She was clearly elated, and called her men to thank God for the victory. And yet she herself could not help grieving for those soldiers who died without having confessed. She wept.[12]

The next day was Ascension Thursday, a day of rest. Joan did not put on her armor. This did not, however, stop either the French commanders from meeting and discussing future plans, or Joan from issuing the order for all the men who wanted to fight on Friday to confess. It is reported that "it was done as Joan ordered."[13] Nor did it stop her from sending the English yet another letter: the third. She had it tied to an arrow and shot over the wall. The reason for the uncommon method of transportation was that the English had, in defiance of all courtesy and the laws of war, detained her herald Guyenne, whom she had sent with her second letter of warning to the English command several days earlier.

What Thursday's plans were, whether Joan took part in laying them, or what Joan's assigned role in them was, is not exactly clear. A rather late chronicler claims that Joan did not take part in the original meeting, but was only called upon after the council had come to its decision in order to be assigned her role, which the chronicler claims was secondary. Joan was to lead a diversionary force against the fort of St. Laurent, whereas the main attack was to be against the fort of St.-Jean-de-Blanc. The chronicler adds that the council attempted to keep from her the fact that there were to be two assaults. Their attempt, it's reported, was not successful. Joan quickly unmasked their real plans, after having once again let them brush against her temper.[14] This account does not, however, seem trustworthy, not only because Friday's attack did not include a diversion but also because one would expect Wednesday's events to have taught the Armagnac commanders that Joan was not easily fooled.

Whatever Thursday's plans were, Friday's events don't clarify them in the least unless, of course, those plans were contradictory. Joan rose early, confessed and took communion. At 9:00 in the morning Joan, Dunois, La Hire, Gilles de Rais, and other Franco-Armagnac commanders, rode out of the gate of Bourgogne leading a force of some four thousand men.

Franco-Armagnac troops made for the Loire, forded it to the Île des Toiles, and crossed over to the southern bank of the river using a pontoon bridge. Their objective was the bastille of St.-Jean-le-Blanc, which was the next smallest of the English forts. Fording rivers and crossing pontoon bridges takes time, however, and the English were quick to understand the Franco-Armagnacs' objective. They were too few to put up a serious fight against them. As the Franco-Armagnacs crossed the river, as such, the Anglo-Burgundian troops in St. Jean made for their larger monastery-turned-fort, the Augustins.

The French reconnaissance party's response was to turn on its heels. They were terrified. They felt that they were too few to take the larger fort. All of the French troops who had already crossed the river followed suit. They had, it seems, received the order to retreat. The English response was to storm out of the Augustins and attack the retreating French army.

At that moment, Joan and La Hire finished crossing the river. When they saw the English attack the rearguard of their army, they couched their lances and charged against them. Joan called her soldiers to "go boldly in the name of the Lord."[15] Thereupon the retreating Armagnac forces disregarded their orders, turned on their heels, and attacked the English. The fury of their response was such that they not only forced the English back into the fort, but forced them out of it. They took the fort by assault. It was a quick victory. The English soldiers who survived the assault fled to the largest and most important of their forts, the Tourelles.

After dinner that evening Joan received a message from the council of war. Once again, fear took possession of the commanders. The captains of the Franco-Armagnac army had had a meeting and decided to delay further attacks. They had, after all, had a great victory and thanked God for it, but they felt that their numbers were too small to complete their mission and raise the siege altogether. And since Orléans was well provisioned at last, (above and beyond the food that the relief forces had brought with them—the army had found a large quantity of food at the Augustins), they decided to wait for reinforcements. Joan responded that as the captains had their counsel, so too did she, and hers would last. She then turned to Pasquerel, her confessor, and told him that they would have to rise very early the next morning, earlier than they had that morning. For she would be wounded in battle on the morrow, and "blood would flow from above her breast." [16]

There was a showdown the next morning. Joan made for the gate of Bourgogne, after having heard mass, donned her armor, and refused some shad for breakfast. There she ran into the bailiff of Orléans, Raoul of Gaucourt, who informed her that there would be no fighting that day. He had men blocking the gate. Joan responded that will he, or nill he, French troops would fight that day, and conquer.[17] She called for her troops. The town militia who were gathered there, including those blocking the gate, responded to her orders with joy. They formed ranks and marched with such vehemence that Gaucourt later claimed that his having attempted to stop Joan had put his life in danger.[18]

Joan made for the Tourelles, the most important of the forts in English hands—it controlled the bridge spanning the Loire. Her orders had roused more than just the soldiers. The Franco-Armagnac captains also marched on that day. They all met at the Augustins, where they laid plans for the assault. They decided to attack the fort from three directions simultaneously. The battle lasted till sunset.

Early on in the battle Joan, who was the first person of her group to step on a scaling ladder, was wounded by an arrow that pierced her shoulder near the neck, and was carried off the battlefield. Joan was frightened. Her armor was taken off. Some of her men, who saw that she was wounded, offered her a charm for the wound. Joan refused it saying, "I would rather die than do what I know to be a sin, or to be against God's law."[19] They settled instead for putting olive oil and pig's grease on the wound and binding it with cotton to stop the flow of blood.

It is remarkable that none of the soldiers who saw her wound was in the least bit aroused by the sight, even though Joan breasts were, as the duke d'Alençon put it, beautiful. Nor did the men who lived with Joan in close quarters during her glorious ascent ever feel sexually aroused by her. Several remarked as such, claiming that they feared and respected her too much.[20]

The fighting continued, but it seemed ineffectual and interminable. The English put up a strenuous defense. "They fought as though they were immortal," was the way a contemporary chronicler put it.[21] Twice in the course of that day French commanders approached Joan—who was wounded and no longer on the battlefield—and tried to postpone the attack. The first time was around midday. Dunois made for Joan with the recommendation that the fighting be put off until the next day. Joan would not hear of it. She suggested that the men be fed and ordered them to continue the assault since the English "could not last much longer."[22] The second time was at sunset. Retreat had been sounded when Dunois approached Joan once again, repeating his request. He relates that Joan responded by getting up, grabbing her horse, and riding to a nearby vineyard where she started to pray. Eight minutes later she emerged from the vineyard, mounted her horse, seized her standard, and galloped to her men, calling them to make one last assault.[23]

That last assault won the day. The French—including that part of the militia which had been left behind to defend the city—utterly destroyed the English forces in the Tourelles. Over five hundred English soldiers died, and all of the very few survivors taken prisoner. The cathedral bells rang the *Te Deum*.

On the following day, which was a Sunday, what was left of the Anglo-Burgundian garrisons at Orléans emerged from their forts with the intent, it seems, of staging one last battle. They hoped to make up for their losses. They set up in full battle formation, archers and all, baiting the Franco-Armagnacs. Joan, Dunois, and the other captains responded by mimicking the English. They placed their army in battle formation directly in front of their adversaries, waiting for the attack. But the English did not attack. The French, who had finally vanquished their fear, wanted to take the initiative and charge against the English. It was Joan who stopped them. She would not stand for fighting on Sunday, she said, unless it was for defensive purposes.[24] She was also keenly aware of the fact that the English had a decided advantage in battles of the sort that they proposed on that day. Drawn in full battle formation, the English troops were very dangerous. After a standoff lasting an hour, the English simply retreated. Orléans was free.

Right: **Joan of Arc. Paris, France.** (Courtesy Vanni/Art Resource, NY)

Below: **Joan of Arc before the king. From a printed edition of** *Vigiles de Charles VII.* (Courtesy Snark/Art Resource, NY)

Right: **At the castle of Loches, Joan announces the delivery of Orléans to King Charles VII.** (Courtesy Erich Lessing/Art Resource, NY

6

From Jargeau to Meung

Do not have doubts. When God pleases, the hour is ripe.
—*Joan of Arc*

NEWS OF THE VICTORY AT ORLÉANS quickly spread throughout
France. The dauphin and the Franco-Armagnacs began to feel a
sense of great relief and new confidence. The Anglo-Burgundians,
on the other hand, were in a general state of shock at the reawak-
ening of the French. They were above all terrified of Joan.
Legends about her magical powers had already begun to spread in
their camp. The incident with Joan's herald Guyenne shows just
how much those legends had grown.

Following the dictates of medieval warfare, Joan had sent the
commanders of the English troops garrisoned at Orléans three letters of warning before her attempt to raise the siege of Orléans actually began. The first one was written up at Poitiers. The second she
sent by way of her two heralds, Guyenne and Ambleville, while she
was waiting for Dunois to return to Orléans with reinforcements.
The third one she had shot at the end of an arrow over the wall of
one of the English forts. She hadn't sent her third message by herald because the English commanders had not respected her heralds'
immunity. The English response to Joan's second missive had been
to detain Guyenne, which was a direct violation of protocol.

Ambleville reported that the English kept Guyenne in order to burn him. Joan replied to Ambleville, assuring him that in God's name they would do his companion no harm, and bidding him to go boldly back to the English, for no harm would befall him either, and he would bring back his companion safe and sound.[1]

When Joan's troops completed the liberation of Orléans, they found her herald safe and sound, albeit in chains.[2] But this was not because the English were not prepared to carry out their threats. They had already prepared the stake for him and had sent to the University of Paris for its opinion on the matter. They simply had not had the time to do so. They were too busy fighting Joan to burn her herald in her effigy.

The English had every reason to be afraid of Joan. The *Pucelle* of Orléans, as she came to be known after the siege of Orléans had been raised, had done for the French what no one had been able to do in the long years of the Anglo-French feud. She had done what no one, least of all the English, had dreamt was possible: She had united the French, by giving them hope, strength, and a mission. She had singlehandedly reopened a matter, which everyone—the English above all—believed settled: that the English would take over the throne of France.

The events of Orléans make this very clear. Before Joan arrived, the citizens of Orléans were ready to surrender. They had even attempted to do so—and not because they were starving, or because their lives were in great danger. Orléans had attempted to surrender because active resistance seemed pointless to them. What was there to be gained from resistance? It merely delayed what seemed to be an inevitable event: their falling under English supremacy. After the royal house of France signed the Treaty of Troyes, the French crown seemed destined to belong to one of the Henrys of England, because there was nothing that could really challenge that treaty. Franco-Armagnac resistance had been completely ineffective. But when Joan emerged from the "marches of Lorraine," the Franco-Armagnacs dared to hope that there was a way out of their predicament—and that the throne of France could remain in French hands. And with their hope came strength and the will to fight for their cause.

The militia certainly felt the effects of Joan's presence immediately. The Franco-Armagnac commanders were so accustomed to losing before Joan appeared that they had decided not to descend onto the battlefield until they were absolutely sure of having sufficient numbers to crush the English. French morale was so low before Joan appeared that the Franco-Armagnacs even lost those battles in which they outnumbered the Anglo-Burgunians on a massive scale. More often than not, they simply preferred to stay off the battlefield. The attack on the Tourelles is the most clamorous example of this. After having won battles for two consecutive days, the commanders simply did not have the courage to try their "luck" for a third day in a row. They were willing to give up their obvious advantage in order to postpone the battle.

Joan immediately changed the Franco-Armagnac mood. She forced the Franco-Armagnac commanders to fight. Day after day she gave the soldiers the will to do so. For Joan won the battles she forced the Franco-Armagnac resistance to fight, and the victories gave the soldiers the confidence they needed to win. It was the soldiers who eventually helped her tip the scales. When Joan called for the attack on the Tourelles, it was the militia that responded to her orders—with joy.

It wasn't only in the militia that Joan made a difference. Once she appeared, the people of France began to become involved in the fight for their freedom. It is once again the events at Orléans that give the true measure of this. The mood in Orléans changed when Joan entered its gates. People rushed to her "making as much rejoicing as if they had seen God descend in their midst; and not without cause, for they had many cares, travails and difficulties and, worse than this, great fear lest they lose all, body and goods."[3]

The people of Orléans didn't flock to Joan simply to pay her homage. They flocked to her to fight with her. They flocked to her to fight for her. They followed her on her sorties outside the walls of their town, even though this meant emerging from the safety of their walls and putting their lives at risk. They took part in their militia's battles against the English forts. They quartered the militia Joan had brought with her with good cheer—which was a rare thing indeed. The Orléannais all wanted to be an active part of Joan's quest.

And just as Joan had made the difference in Orléans, just as she had transformed a despondent town into an aggressive one, so too did she risk doing so in all of France. After Joan had raised the siege on the town of Orléans, Franco-Armagnac nobility was willing to mortgage its properties to raise troops, and the people of France began to attack the English soldiers garrisoned in their midst. This was something which the Anglo-Burgundians definitely did not want.

Joan, on the other hand, who knew from the start that "she would not last for more than a year," was eager to put that year to good use. The Anglo-Burgundians still controlled most of northern France; they still held Guyenne in southwestern France; the duke of Orléans was still in English hands; and Charles of Valois, the dauphin, had as yet to be crowned.

Joan left Orléans on May 9, the day after her victory, and made for Tours and the dauphin. With her were Dunois, Gilles de Rais, La Hire, and a large part of their army. Their intent was to collect more troops so that they could continue the fight while the English were still in a state of shock. They did not, however, agree on the next step to be taken in their campaign. The captains of the Orléans victory felt that the best tactic was to attack the Anglo-Burgundians in those parts of France which were solidly in their hands. They therefore proposed to continue the fight in Normandy, which was an English stronghold. Joan, on the other hand, wanted to accompany the dauphin to Reims, where French kings had been crowned since 1026, and have him crowned. She felt that the coronation would sanction Charles's claim to the throne. Coronations were a sacred thing in the Middle Ages. The two plans were not mutually exclusive. Both entailed going north with the army; both entailed reconquering lands held by the Anglo-Burgundians; both were very aggressive plans. It would not have been too terribly difficult to find a compromise between the two.

But the dauphin's council dismissed a northern venture altogether. They proposed that the Franco-Armagnac forces complete their liberation of those castles and towns on the Loire, which the English had seized in their offensive in October of the previous year, before they made any attempt to attack the lion in his den. Theirs was a more cautious and diplomatic suggestion. From the diplomatic point of view, freeing the Loire towns did not entail an out-and-out attack on the duke of Burgundy. The duke had pulled out of the English attack on the Loire in February of 1429. This meant that Burgundy could not take offense at a Franco-Armagnac attack on the forces garrisoned there. This was important to the dauphin's council, which seemed more interested in not rocking the boat than it was in liberating France.

From the tactical point of view, on the other hand, the liberation of the Loire towns was simply much less of a risk than an open attack on the Anglo-Burgundian strongholds in northern France. It therefore put Charles's own reputation less at risk. For in the unhappy event that Joan's was simply a single fortunate victory, it would look much less disastrous for the dauphin if she were subsequently defeated in a minor battle, than it would if she defeated in a full-scale Franco-Armagnac attack on the Anglo-Burgundians. The size of the next battle, in other words, was a measure of the belief that Charles placed in Joan. Lastly, the towns on the Loire also happened to be on those English-held lands which were closest to the dauphin's personal holdings. To oust the English from these lands meant removing the personal threat to Charles.

Of the three objectives, the Normandy proposal was immediately rejected. It was the most aggressive. What was decided upon was a compromise between Joan's proposal and the dauphin's council's. The dauphin would be crowned in Reims after the castles and towns on the Loire had been freed. Reaching that compromise took precious time. The dauphin made Joan wait some two weeks before he personally received her to discuss the next move to be made. This may not have been completely due to ill will on his part; after all, he was overjoyed by the news from Orléans, and Joan herself needed some time to heal from her wound. In all probability, however, political concerns also played a part in his decision. The dauphin seems to have wanted the elation of his troops and commanders to ebb before speaking to Joan.

Joan and Charles of Valois met at Tours, where the debate on the next target was breached, but not resolved. The debate was carried on to Loches, where the royal entourage had headed when it left Tours. Loches held another of the dauphin's beloved castles. At Loches, Joan implored the dauphin to ride with her to be crowned. She knelt and clasped his knees begging him to believe that she could see to it that he was crowned.[4]

But Joan wasn't the only person to hold the dauphin's ear. She had his council to contend with. The dauphin's council asked Joan if it was upon her counsel's suggestion that she proposed that the Franco-Armagnac forces make for Reims. Joan replied that it was. At which the royal council, who no doubt had many reasons for wanting to downplay Joan's suggestion, asked her how the voices communicated with her. It was the dauphin who urged Joan to respond to the question. Joan replied by telling them: "that when something was not going well because people would not leave it to her to follow the counsel that was sent her from God, she would retire apart and pray to God, complaining to Him that the men to whom she spoke would not readily believe in her. And when she had prayed to God, she heard a voice which said to her: 'Go, child of God, go, go! Go, and I will help you.' And when she heard this voice she felt a great joy, and wanted to be in that state always."[5]

That remarkable reply, which was as much a description of Joan's experiences as it was a warning to the council and an indication of Joan's impatience with their indecisiveness, convinced the dauphin to heed Joan's request to lead him to Reims. Intent as he may have been on Joan's quest, however, the dauphin could not drown out his own political interests. He also agreed with his council, and understood the implications of their suggestion to liberate the Loire area. On May 23, when he finally communicated his decision, he declared that he approved of both suggestions—Joan's and his council's—and would make for Reims as soon as the Loire had been freed. He named his cousin Jean d'Alençon—who had finally paid off his ransom (largely by selling his and his wife's lands[6]) and was therefore once again free to fight—lieutenant general of his armies with the provision that he follow Joan's advice in all things.

Joan and d'Alençon, whom Joan called her *beau duc*, or handsome duke, had become very close friends during her first visit at Chinon, when, taken aback by her skill on the tilting field, he had given her the charger. While they were waiting for the dauphin to decide upon the best course of action for the royal armies, d'Alençon and Joan went to the abbey of Saint Florent to meet his wife and mother, to whom Joan promised that he would return safely from the war. D'Alençon, as such, did what the royal decree demanded of him with joy. He followed Joan's advice "as one who took great pleasure at seeing her in his company."[7] On June 9, d'Alençon, Joan, and a large part of the royal army entered Orléans, which was to be the headquarters for their Loire campaign. They planned attacks on Jargeau, Meung, and Beaugency. It would take only nine days for them to sweep, through English domination of the Loire.

Joan, d'Alençon and six thousand lances—roughly two thousand troops—left for Jargeau on the morning after the day they arrived, and spent the night in the woods near the town. They were met there by Dunois, Florent d'Illiers, and some two thousand more troops, who arrived on the morning of June 11. Dunois and d'Alençon were hesitant that morning. Fastolf was on the move once again, and Dunois, once again, felt it best to wait for reinforcements before attempting to attack Jargeau. And it was Joan, once again, who helped the French captains defeat their fear. She informed them that if she weren't sure that it was God who was conducting their campaign, she would be tending her sheep, rather than putting her life in danger; but that since it was God who was conducting their campaign, they should not fear numbers.[8] They settled on an immediate attack of the suburbs of Jargeau.

The English responded to their sally by storming out of the walls of Jargeau and sending the Franco-Armagnac army in flight. Upon seeing her troops retreat, Joan grabbed her standard and led a counterattack, driving the English back into the town walls of Jargeau. The French proceeded to lay siege to the town, bombarding it throughout the rest of the day and night. On the morning of June 12, the English were ready to negotiate. La Hire was approached by the earl of Suffolk, the commander of the English garrison at Jargeau, who wanted a fifteen-day truce, at the end of which he claimed he would surrender the town. His offer had two conditions: that he receive no reinforcements in those fifteen days and, that his men could keep their weapons upon his surrender.

The offer was a ridiculous one. Both the French and the English knew that Fastolf was close by, and therefore that he would arrive before the fifteen days had passed. The truce was merely a half-hearted English attempt to convince the French to give up their obvious advantage. The French took it to be such and turned it down. Joan added that upon their surrender, the English troops in Jargeau could leave the town unharmed, only if they were stripped down to their doublets and tunics.

The fighting resumed shortly after the parley. It was Joan, d'Alençon remembered years later, who ensured that it did. He did not quite have the courage to order the attack. So after having grabbed her standard and calling for the attack, she repeated to him more quietly "Forward, beau duc." And since he thought that it was "premature to attack so quickly," Joan added: "Do not have doubts—when God pleases, the hour is ripe. . . . beau duc, are you afraid? Don't you know that I have promised your wife to bring you back safe and sound?"[9]

Joan kept her promise of watching over d'Alençon's life. At the beginning of their attack, she turned to her beau duc and told him that he had better change vantage points, because a cannon ball would rip through the spot he had chosen in a matter of minutes. He did as he was told, and it happened just as she foretold. The ball hit a M. de Ludes, who was unfortunate enough not to have heard (or perhaps even heeded) the warning.

The French swiftly moved toward Jargeau's walls, past the moats, and raised their ladders to scale them. Joan herself ran to one of the ladders with her standard, only to be hit on the head with a rock when she was halfway up. She fell but quickly got up calling others to follow her because the English were doomed. Jargeau fell within the hour. Eleven hundred English troops were killed that day; the prisoners were taken to Orléans by barge; the English provisions were sacked.[10]

Joan and her army, with the exception of a garrison which they left behind in Jargeau, returned to Orléans with the news that very day. The townspeople thronged to the streets upon their arrival, shouting with joy, acclaiming the victors, and pushing to try to touch the Maid, the soldier, who had dispelled their worst nightmares. Joan was quickly becoming a legend. Even the duke of Orléans, who was being held hostage in England, arranged to give her a token of his appreciation. Upon her arrival in Orléans, Joan received a cape and cap in the colors of the house of Orléans sent by the duke.[11]

Joan, on the other hand, had no time to waste in receiving honors. Her army was growing rapidly. Volunteers of all sorts and from all parts of France flocked to her.[12] Such was becoming the size of her army that it could not be sheltered within the walls of Orléans.

Many of the new recruits had to sleep in the fields outside the town. Besides, Joan had other cities to free. On the evening of the fourteenth, shortly after vespers, she approached d'Alençon and told him to prepare the troops. They would march for Meung on the morning of the very next day.

It was a short march. Meung was only fifteen miles west of Orléans. This gave Joan and her men the time to capture the bridge at Meung on the very day of their arrival. On June 16, she sent half of her men ahead to Beaugency, five miles further west. The latter troops captured the town without even having to fight for it. As they approached the town, the English troops garrisoned there retreated to the southern banks of the Loire and into the castle controlling the town's bridge.

Joan's plans had become more ambitious. The reasoning behind her move is clear—to attack enemy forces while they were divided. Rather than giving her enemies the chance to stage a joint venture, she simply cut off communication between them. The French knew that they were soon to have a third English force to contend with; Fastolf was indeed on the move. They therefore had to clean up the area quickly, before the towns' garrisons were reinforced.

On the sixteenth, as such, the French held Beaugency, while the English were stuck in the castle guarding the town's bridge, whereas the English held Meung, with the French garrisoned in the tower controlling that town's bridge. Fastolf finally arrived that day, with some five thousand relief troops. They stopped at Janville, a town ten miles north of Beaugency, which had served as English headquarters throughout their Loire campaign. So too, however, did Richemont, the constable of France, who was nominally, at least, in charge of the dauphin's military affairs, arrive with some two thousand reinforcement troops for the French.

Numbers were not the only thing that distinguished the arrival of these two sets of reinforcement troops. There was a political problem behind the French reinforcement. Richemont had fallen out of the dauphin's favor, and the dauphin had expressly forbidden him to take part in the liberation of the Loire. Joan's captains were therefore very nervous about admitting him in their ranks, however useful his troops might have been. Fortunately for the French, Joan was not interested in political factions. Rather than paying any attention to internal feuds, she simply approached the constable and bid him welcome: "Noble constable, you have not come through any act of mine, but since you have come, you shall be welcome."[13]

The English, on the other hand, had a problem of communications. The garrisons stationed at Meung and Beaugency were on opposite sides of the Loire, and the French had effectively cut them off from one another. For all intents and purposes, Joan's troops controlled both of the towns' bridges. The bridge at Meung was theirs, which meant that the English garrison at Meung could not cross over to the southern bank of the Loire. They also held the northern entrance of the bridge at Beaugency, which meant that the English troops there could only receive relief from the southern bank of the Loire. The garrison in the worst shape was the one in Beaugency; Fastolf's troops were on the northern bank of the Loire.

Beaugency capitulated on the seventeenth, and the surrendering garrison was allowed to leave with its weapons. That evening Fastolf's troops and the French at Beaugency met face to face some two miles north of the town. The English were expecting a fight. They set up in battle formation just as they had at Orléans, baiting Joan's troops to attack. Joan, however, did not want to fight that evening, or at least not in that way. She was no fool. The French had lost most of the battles in which they attacked the English when they were in full battle formation, even those in which they outnumbered the English three to one. (Twenty thousand or so French soldiers lost to seven thousand English soldiers at the battle of Agincourt.) Just as she had in Orléans, Joan held back her men, bidding her enemies to get some rest, and adding that "God willing," they would fight the next day.[14]

The English retired to Meung, where they bombarded the bridge all night in hopes of gaining control of it and getting some help over to the garrison stranded in Beaugency. They clearly had not heard that that garrison had already surrendered. In the morning, they learned that there was no more garrison at Beaugency. Their curious response was to leave Meung altogether. Their objective was clearly similar to Joan's on the previous evening—to postpone the fighting until they had the field advantage. Experience had shown them that Joan's specialty was assaulting towns.

The French had, therefore, freed the Loire, but not solved their real problem. They needed to defeat the English army before it could return to attack them. Their problem, as it turned out, was harder to solve than they had at first imagined it would be. They could not find their foe. Once Joan discovered that the English had left, she called for a chase. Theirs would be an easy victory, she claimed. She was sure of it: "She was certain and knew in truth that the English, their enemies, were waiting to fight them; and she added that, in the name of God, people should ride against them, and that they would be beaten. Some then asked where the English were to be found; to which she answered: 'Ride boldly on, and you will have a good guide.'" [15]

A large group of trackers, some sixty or seventy men who were reputed to be the best and most ferocious Armagnac riders, led by La Hire, was sent to find the vanishing English. The main body of the army, led by Dunois and d'Alençon, followed close behind. The chase lasted for quite some time. The Armagnac army almost caught up to the English at Meung but quickly lost track of them. Oddly enough, both the army in pursuit and the army in flight headed in the same direction—towards Patay. It was in the woods that surrounded the town that the Armagnac trackers caught up to the English rearguard. The problem was that they did not know it.

The woods around Patay were full of soldiers that day. The French were frantically looking for the English. The English were trying desperately not to be found. Had their situation not had lethal consequences, the whole scene would have been enormously funny.

It was the English who first caught sight of the French and began to set up their battle formation. This should have given them the day. The French did not even suspect that the English had seen them at that point, and could therefore not have been in the least bit aware of their enemy's maneuvers. Nor would they ever have known of those maneuvers, until of course it was too late, had it not been for a stag, which ran through the English camp just when the English were driving their stakes into the ground. The English started to chase down the stag. The noise of the chase alerted the French who discovered just how close their foes were and attacked them before they had managed to complete their fortifications and unleash their terrible archers.

The battle was quickly over. Almost all of the English—some four thousand men—were killed and their captains taken prisoner. The one exception was Fastolf himself, who to his great shame managed to escape under a white flag and with a small company.[16] The French lost three men, on the most pessimistic of counts. The battle ended so quickly that Joan barely made it to the field in time to dismount from her horse, gather a dying Englishman in her arms, and hear his confession.

Joan and her troops returned to Orléans, after having spent the night in the town of Patay. Everyone expected Charles of Valois, in whose name the army had reaped its victories, to join in the victory celebration at Orléans. But Charles never came. He sat in Sully, the castle of Georges de La Trémoïlle.

The aftermath of Patay was panic on the Anglo-Burgundian side. The English commander of the garrison at Janville, the once-headquarters of the Anglo-Burgundian Loire expedition, quickly swore allegiance to the dauphin. Other English garrisons along the Loire, on the other hand, fled to Paris. Paris was in a frenzy at that time, expecting Joan's army to head north.

Above: **Charles VII, a ruthless and subtle king, is generally misunderstood as one of history's fools.** (Courtesy Giraudon/Art Resources, NY)

Right: **Franco-Flemish 15th c. Portrait of Joan of Arc.** (Courtesy Giraudon/Art Resources, NY)

7

Reims

Good king, now is executed the will of God.

—*Joan of Arc*

WHATEVER JOAN'S ENEMIES might have thought, what was paramount in Joan's mind at that point was not Paris, but the coronation. Her voices had been adamant on the matter. For Joan had to reestablish the "Blood Royal," as she had put it in her letter to the commanders of the English garrisons at Orléans, and that was a two-part quest. It entailed liberating France from the English and unifying the people of France under Charles of Valois's kingship.

The tasks were equally difficult and important. For as difficult as it was to vanquish the English invaders, it was just as difficult to unite the French, who had been at war with each other since the assassination of the duke of Orléans in 1407. And as crucial as defeating the English was to giving Charles of Valois kingship over France, convincing the people of France that Charles was their king was just as crucial to that end. The dauphin could never have truly become king of the French without popular consent.

Hence the urgency of the coronation. Crowning the dauphin would help Joan attain both of these objectives. Anointing was, after all, a sacred rite in the Middle Ages, and was perceived by the people as being such. Joan expected the people of France would immediately acknowledge that Charles of Valois was their true sovereign, once he was anointed and crowned. As for the English, Joan claimed that, "once the king was crowned and anointed the power of his enemies would decline continually until finally they would be powerless to harm either him or his country."[1]

The dauphin was just as urgent as Joan was on the matter of his coronation. After the victory of Patay, he set out for Gien, which was the ideal place from which to depart for Reims, and with what looks like haste, at least by his standards. He arrived there on June 23—only four days after the battle of Patay.

By that time Joan had over ten thousand troops with which she gladly marched to Gien, where she arrived two days later, on June 25. Joan was clearly expecting to make for Reims at once. She was painfully aware of the fact that she had very little time to accomplish everything she was called to do. Rapid departures were not, however, in the dauphin's—or his council's—style. Once Joan's army had arrived in Gien, the council decided to delay—or perhaps even to thwart—the trip, despite the plans that had been laid at Loches a month earlier before Joan had left for the Loire expedition.

Once Joan saw that the council intended to renegotiate the Loches agreement it had made with the captains of the royal army, she promptly intervened. She knew how dangerous it was to let French noblemen stew in their doubts. She therefore tried to impress upon the dauphin the importance of the coronation itself and got the people of France involved in preparations for it. She had the coronation announced in Orléans and in Tours. Above all, she told the dauphin not to worry about the military details of the coronation journey. She pointed out that they did not risk being stranded in Anglo-Burgundian-held lands, as the council had said. For her already sizable army would quickly grow. They would, as such, have numbers on their side.

And so it happened. Men came from all parts of France to fight with Joan.[3] They were even willing to fight without being paid, just to be at her side. "For everyone had great hopes that by means of this Joan much good would befall the kingdom of France, and wished and

The Dauphin's Court

The council's primary fear, or so it claimed, was for the dauphin's safety. Reims is in the heart of Champagne, which was securely held by the Anglo-Burgundians at that time. Approaching it, as such, meant conquering enemy territory, and perhaps even putting the dauphin's life in danger. The council therefore wanted to postpone the coronation. It proposed an alternative task for Joan's army. Instead it should conquer the most important towns on the Loire which were still in Anglo-Burgundian hands: La Charité and Cosne. The latter venture would also have entailed a direct attack on the duke of Burgundy (La Charité is in Burgundy). It would not, however, have endangered the dauphin's life.

The council's fear for Charles's life may have been genuine. What is certain, however, is that the dauphin's safety was not their primary concern. What the councilors—Georges de La Trémoïlle, foremost among them—feared more was losing their ascendancy over the dauphin himself. Charles of Valois was a man of shifting affections. There was always a *favorite* in his court—a person on whom he focused his attention and by whose will he was apparently dominated—and that favorite had

a way of being replaced.

The Richemont episode is a classic example. Before Richemont (the constable of France who joined Joan at Orléans for the nine-day sweep of the Loire) was banished from Charles's court, he had been Charles's favorite, and for quite some time. On a very unfortunate day for him, however, he presented La Trémoïlle to the dauphin, urging his prince to make good use of his friend's considerable skills. La Trémoïlle was not really a newcomer to the dauphin's court, when Richemont did him the favor. He had been lurking in the sidelines at the court for some time, waiting for his chance to emerge. He knew the rules of Charles's game. So when Richemont finally gave him the chance to meet Charles face to face, he knew how to take advantage of the opportunity, and bring an end to the Richemont ascendancy. When Charles's attentions turned to him, as they always did when Charles met someone new, he made sure those attentions remained polarized by convincing the dauphin to banish Richemont.

Charles's was, therefore, a nervous council. Everyone in the council knew that La Trémoïlle would eventually be replaced by a new favorite, and they all feared that that new favorite might be Joan. And that not because a shift in favorites would bring about another palace revolution—a shift in the powers of the court. They were accustomed to that. They were afraid because the specific shift to Joan risked destroying their particular brand of palace politics altogether. For Joan knew nothing about, and cared even less for, their kind of court politics. As driven as she was, she could not be coaxed into playing the court game of promoting personal interests, of increasing one's wealth, honor, and prestige. Unlike the common court player's, Joan's was not a personal venture. Joan had a quest, and that quest involved the greater good of France. If Joan came to power, if she became the favorite, she would ruin their game. The council knew that if Charles polarized toward Joan, he would become caught up in her quest. And if that happened, they would all lose their place at court.

When the people of France flocked to Joan, as such, the court of councilors began to fear and to loathe Joan. "People said that La Trémoïlle and others of the king's council were very angry that so many [people] came [to Joan], for fear of their own persons."[2] When Joan's renown risked making her the new court favorite, the dauphin's councilors felt that they had to do everything in their power to keep Joan as far away from Charles as they could. This is why they opposed the coronation journey so vehemently. If Charles traveled to Reims, he would necessarily be in close and prolonged contact with Joan at her best and most magnetic, and that was precisely what the council could not afford. Hence they pointed out how dangerous the trip could be, and that there were other things that had to be done for the Franco-Armagnac cause, things that did not require Charles's presence. They were also content to discuss matters. A long, and drawn out discussion on the next move to be made kept matters on their own turf and within their control.

desired to serve her, and know her deeds, as a thing sent by God."[4]

The dauphin listened to Joan's advice but did not act upon it. So it was Joan who made the next move. On June 27, she pulled her troops out of Gien and made for the fields surrounding the town. This was somewhat of a threatening move. With her troops garrisoned outside the town walls, Joan could well have left Gien without the dauphin's consent, or even laid siege to the town itself. Whatever her intentions were, her move hit its mark. The whole party, the dauphin included, left for Reims two days later. Charles sent out invitations for his coronation.

Their first major stop was Auxerre, where they arrived on July 1. The town, which was firmly in Anglo-Burgundian hands, refused to open its gates to Joan and her dauphin. This put the coronation party at odds once again. Joan and her captains wanted to force the town to capitulate and swear allegiance to the dauphin; the dauphin and his council—which always kept a close eye on Joan—preferred to parley.

Joan was held in check. Her army moved on once Auxerre had issued a very conditional surrender. The town would swear fealty to the dauphin once Troyes, Châlon, and Reims had. It did, however, sell the coronation party those supplies which it needed to continue its march, and give the dauphin's favorite counselor, La Trémoïlle, a two-thousand-crown bribe for keeping Joan off the battlefield.[5]

They marched on to St. Florentin, a smaller town which surrendered immediately, and on to Troyes where they arrived on July 5, greeted by three cannon shots from the Anglo-Burgundian soldiers garrisoned there. Troyes's gates too were closed. The councilmen of Troyes had heard that Auxerre had avoided giving an unconditional surrender by playing to the diplomatic side of the dauphin's entourage, and hoped to do the same.

Deliberation in Charles's camp began anew. A meeting of the dauphin's council and war captains was called. Joan was conspicuously absent. The meeting ended in a stalemate: The council called for a complete retreat from Burgundian lands; the war captains insisted on attacking Troyes. One of the two options had to be chosen quickly. Joan's army was very large, by the standards of the day, and the coronation party was running short of food.

At that point Joan was summoned. When she arrived, she asked the dauphin if he was finally ready to believe in her and grant what she was about to request. Charles replied that he would most willingly trust her if she proposed some viable way out of the predicament. Joan responded by asking for three days' time, at the end of which she guaranteed that Troyes would capitulate. "Noble dauphin, command your people to come and besiege the city of Troyes, and drag out your debates no longer. For in God's name, within three days I will lead you into the city of Troyes, by love, force, or courage, and that false Burgundy will be quite thunderstruck." The dauphin granted her that much.

Joan set to work immediately and feverishly. She posted her men outside the town's walls, arming them with the heavy artillery the coronation party had brought with it; having them make large bundles of sticks with which to fill the town's moats; and laying out the strategy with which her forces would assault the town. Dunois later commented that "the most famous and experienced captains would not have made so good a plan of battle."[6] In a day and a half Joan was ready to stage the attack.

Troyes's citizens had a good view of Joan's activities from the walls of their town. These preparations must have looked ominous, especially since the town militia was insignificant in comparison to the army they saw outside their town. They panicked. The town council hurried to find a solution to their troubles. Their deliberation was not lengthy: "Trembling," they surrendered immediately after Joan had sounded the attack. Charles issued a general pardon to the townspeople for their resistance. The Anglo-Burgundian garrison retreated armed and unharmed; its officers even tried to take their prisoners-of-war with them.

Joan was shocked at their lack of chivalry. Her letting the Anglo-Burgundians leave unharmed was generous enough. Their attempting to leave with their prisoners of war was, in her opinion, a decided abuse of her generosity—especially since their prisoners of war were Franco-Armagnac. She rushed to the gate from which they were about to leave "declaring that in God's name, they should not carry them off." The Anglo-Burgundians laughed at her naiveté. Their laughter might have sparked her temper had Charles not intervened, and paid the Anglo-Burgundians their prisoners' ransoms.[7]

Joan had a surprising ally in her victory at Troyes, a Franciscan friar named Brother Richard, who, like Savonarola, was a very famous doomsday preacher. He had drawn enormous crowds in Paris in the spring of 1429 for a series of sermons on the precariousness of worldly delights. His variations on the *vanity of vanities* had so mesmerized Paris that spring, that a large group of Parisians set fire to their backgammon boards, cards, dice, and luxurious garments after one of his sermons. Richard was also an Armagnac, and had foretold the arrival of a great wonder, who would soon change the French scene.

But Brother Richard's Parisian success was to be short lived. Once the local civil and university authorities found out about him and his political affiliations, they informed him that they were keeping an eye on him. So Richard left quietly in the night and headed toward Champagne, leaving a large crowd of unhappy people in Paris.

Brother Richard approached Joan on the night of her arrival. At her Rouen trial Joan recounted that he was at first a bit wary of her. He made the sign of the cross, splashed her with holy water, and proceeded to recite the prayer to "St. Michael the Archangel," in order to exorcise evil spirits which may have flitted around her. Joan laughed and told him to approach boldly—she would not "fly away." Brother Richard responded by falling to his knees. Joan joined him and fell to hers.[8] Satisfied by her response, Brother Richard returned to Troyes and urged the townspeople to surrender to Joan and the dauphin. Joan and the dauphin rode side by side into Troyes on the morning of July 10, with the army following on their heels.

Their pace quickened after Troyes. The coronation party had almost reached its destination. They arrived in Châlons-sur-Marne on July 14. The good citizens of Châlons, who had clearly heard from those of Troyes and Auxerre, did not know whose footsteps to follow. The town council considered the Auxerre route the wiser, if not safer, of the two. The councilmen knew, of course, that they could only put up a token resistance—twelve thousand troops was a very large army at the time. What they did not expect to have to resist was their own townspeople, who swarmed out of the gates to greet Joan and the dauphin upon their arrival.[9] Joan's patriotic fever was becoming increasingly contagious. Even the dauphin showed some signs of having caught it at that point. Charles sent out heralds to invite his people to his impending coronation. (Coronations were a public affair at the time.)

The stay at Châlons was very brief. The day after they had arrived, the party made for Sept-Saulx, the castle of the Archbishop of Reims, who had traveled with them since Gien, which they reached on the sixteenth. There they were met by a delegation of men from Reims, who gave the dauphin the keys to their city.[10] Theirs was the first formal unsolicited homage of a major town in the heartland of Anglo-Burgundian territory.

The Anglo-Burgundian garrison which had been stationed at Reims was preparing to set out for Paris when this encounter took place. They had been more or less ousted by the citizens of Reims. The captains of the garrison had called a general assembly of the people of Reims several days earlier, and informed them that resisting the Armagnacs was within their reach if they so wished. All they had to do was hold out for six weeks; English reinforcements would arrive by then.[11] But the people of Reims did not wish to resist. It was not the fear of a siege that led them to open their gates to Joan and the dauphin. Nor was it the thought of the highly improbable six-week resistance to twelve thousand troops. (None of Joan's military offensives had lasted for more than five days at that point.) The Rémois had simply caught Joan's patriotic fever and rejoiced at her arrival.

Charles, Joan, and the army rode into Reims that very evening. The streets were lined with people who came from near and far—both Joan and Charles had summoned the people of France to come to the coronation—who yelled "Noël" to their uncrowned king, as their forefathers had for generations. It was their acknowledgement of his right to be crowned; to sit on what tradition told them was Charlemagne's own throne; to be anointed with the chrism of kings, which legend told them heaven had given St. Rémi to anoint Clovis, the first king of the Franks, after his conversion to Christianity. Both of these legendary events had taken place on Christmas day. Charlemagne was crowned on Christmas day in Rome of the year 800, and Clovis was anointed on Christmas day of the year 496.

It was Saturday. Coronations were traditionally held on Sunday and the untraditional coronation party—Charles's was perhaps the only coronation to have taken place behind enemy lines during a long and difficult war—felt that it was best not to break another rule. So they decided to have the coronation take place the very next day. There were many reasons for their choice. The primary reason was that they did not want to weigh on the backs of the citizens of Reims after they had shown them such a warm welcome. Feeding a twelve-thousand-man army for an entire week was very expensive. This was not, however, the only reason. Reims is very close to both the duchy of Burgundy and to the town of Épernay, the latter of which was teeming with English troops at the time. To linger in Reims for a week might therefore have brought on a battle with the English, who were clearly informed about the coronation, and adverse to it.

The coronation ceremony was long and elaborate and began hours after Charles and Joan had entered Reims. At three o'clock the next morning, the dauphin made for the cathedral, where he kept an all-night vigil, preparing for his incumbent knighthood and coronation. The official ceremony began six hours later.

At nine o'clock, on the morning of Sunday, July 17, 1429, the doors of the cathedral were opened. Four knights of the kingdom made for the chapel of St. Rémy, where the *Sainte Ampoule*, the vial of the holy oil with which the kings of France were anointed, was stored. They were in full armor and bore their standards. They were to be the escort for the abbot of the abbey church of St. Rémy, whose role it was to carry the vial to the archbishop of Reims, who was in the cathedral waiting for it, and would anoint the king with the chrism it contained. After the knights had sworn to protect the Ampoule with their lives and to return it to the abbey, the abbot rode the horse which the dauphin had provided for the procession. The four knights then placed themselves around the abbot and accompanied him on the short ride to the cathedral. They rode under a gold canopy, into the cathedral and up to the altar, where they all dismounted. The abbot then presented the Ampoule to the archbishop, who placed it on the altar and proceeded to bless the royal ornaments.

In the meanwhile, the dauphin took the coronation oath and was knighted by the duke d'Alençon. Tradition dictated that it be the duke of Burgundy to knight the king-to-be-crowned. But not too surprisingly, the duke of Burgundy had decided not to take part in Charles's coronation, even though Joan had sent him a letter of invitation.

After Charles was knighted, the archbishop anointed him with the holy oil and placed the royal crown upon his head. Another concession had to be made for the crown. The traditional crown of the kings of France, which was usually held in the cathedral, was nowhere to be found. The concession was by no means important. The crucial part of the ceremony was the anointing. For to the medieval mind the chrism of the *Sainte Ampoule* conferred God's grace upon the king of France, making him a vicar of Christ, who is "king of the world."

Once Charles had been anointed and crowned, he turned and presented himself to his people, amidst trumpet blasts and cries of *Noël*. The acclaim was so loud that "it seemed the vaults of the Church would split."[12] The twelve peers of the kingdom were then called upon to join the new king on the altar, and those who were present did so. Proxies took the places of those peers who did not attend the ceremony, for there were quite a few who did not. Philip the Good, duke of Burgundy, wasn't the only person missing; Pierre Cauchon, the bishop of Beauvais, had not shown up, and poor Richemont, the constable of France, had received the order not to appear.

Joan stood at Charles's side holding her standard in her hand throughout the coronation rite.[13] Hers was the only standard that was allowed in the cathedral. And when the judges at Rouen asked her why she had carried her standard with her in the cathedral, she retorted, "It had borne the burden, and it was right that it should have the honor." She did admit to the judges, however, that she might not have held the standard throughout the entire coronation ceremony. For, she recalled, Brother Richard was with her at that time, and may have held it too. But what was more important to her was the coronation itself—having Charles anointed with God's chrism and grace before the eyes of the people of France.

And when the Maid saw that the king was consecrated and crowned, she knelt before him in the presence of all the lords, and said to him, embracing him by the knees and weeping hot tears: "Gentle king, now is executed the will of God, who wished that the siege of Orleans should be lifted, and that you should be brought into this city of Reims to receive your holy consecration, thus showing that you are a true king, and he to whom the kingdom of France should belong."[14]

The Siege of Paris (with Joan of Arc). (Courtesy Giraudon/Art Resource, NY)

Here, as in images of Joan after the publication of her trial in the 1840s, she is depicted in accurate historical detail. (Courtesy Giraudon/Art Resource, NY)

8

Paris

I must safeguard the honor of the king.

—*Joan of Arc*

JOAN HAD ACCOMPLISHED A LARGE PART of what she explicitly claimed to have been called to do: Orléans was free, and the dauphin was crowned. In gratitude the new king, Charles VII, made Domrémy and Greux tax exempt in perpetuity.[1] The question of what was to be done next was a perplexing one for Charles. Joan had done the impossible and, she had accomplished what he had not even dared to hope for after he had exiled himself to Bourges, to play the part of the disinherited scion of the royal house of France. Joan had reconquered a good part of his lands and had had him crowned.

But Charles, too, had a will of his own. He had tried to dispose of Joan once before. After the victory at Patay, he had gently let her know that he understood how tired she must feel after such a venture. In all probability, Charles simply could not bear Joan's intensity. Joan had wept on that occasion. But at St. Benoît–sur–Loire, where that encounter had taken place, Joan had not as yet had Charles crowned, as she pointed out in her response to him: "Do not doubt that you will gain your whole kingdom, and will soon be crowned."[2] On that occasion, as such, the dauphin knew that it was best for him to do as Joan wished.

After Reims, things had changed. Not because Joan had succeeded in capturing Charles's heart, as she had so many others.
Nor because Joan had completed her task. But because she had
given Charles "divine" authorization to do as he wished. He was
king. Charles was very aware of the change in his status. So too,
however, was Joan, who began to sense the dawn of betrayal, or at
least the possibility of it. Joan knew that Charles could cut her out
of his world if he wished, and that there was nothing she could do
to stop him from doing so. Joan had made a king. She could not
very well turn around and not treat him like one.

There was a great deal left to be done. The Loire had been substantially freed; a portion of Anglo-Burgundian lands in Champagne
had sworn fealty to the royal house of France; France had an anointed king—a French king. But Paris was still in English hands, as were
Normandy, Guyenne, and most of Champagne; Burgundy was still
an ally of the English crown; France was still a divided land.

Most importantly, it was a land that had begun to feel the yoke
of foreign domination. The immediate result of the coronation was
that town after town, which had been solidly in Anglo-Burgundian
hands, turned around and swore fealty to the new king: Soissons,
Laon, Provins, Château-Thierry, and many others. The people of
France had chosen their king and he was French.

How was their king to respond? Joan and her captains called for
an immediate attack on Paris. The time, they claimed, was ripe for
it. And indeed it was. Christine de Pisan, the great poetess, broke her
long silence and from the convent in which she had exiled herself
when Paris fell into Anglo-Burgundian hands, called the people of
France to follow Joan. For Joan was "God's messenger," his "peace-
bearer." Through her, France's troubles would be brought to an end:

It was found in the history records that she was destined to
accomplish her mission; for more than five hundred years ago,
Merlin, the Sibyl and Bede foresaw her coming, entered her in
their writings as someone who would put an end to France's

troubles, made prophecies about her saying that she would carry the banner in the French wars.[3]

In her was God's love for France made manifest:

It is a fact worth remembering that God should nevertheless have wished (and this is the truth) to bestow such great blessings on France, through a young virgin. And what honor for the French crown, this proof of divine intervention! For all the blessings which God bestows upon it demonstrates how much he favors it.[4]

As events were quickly to prove, the people of France were more than happy to respond to her call.

One would have expected the king to march triumphantly with his army to Paris, and not just because his people were joyfully acclaiming him as king, nor just because Paris was the capital of France, nor just because his army was undefeated until then; but rather, because he had explicitly acknowledged—or perhaps even claimed—that the city was *his*, by allowing himself to be anointed.

That was precisely what Charles did not do. For some obscure reason, he had begun to negotiate– secretly—with the ambassadors sent to him by the duke of Burgundy, even before he was crowned.[5] That parleying intensified in Reims and continued after his coronation. It kept him in Reims for a full four days after his coronation. Above all, it kept the army from doing anything constructive. For Charles's army—as it had to become after he was crowned—had to follow Charles, and Charles had decided to meander.

The new king left Reims on July 21, and proceeded to tend to the sick in the priory of St. Marcoul at Corbigny. It was traditional for a newly crowned king to attempt to cure the scrofulous. It was popularly believed that his anointing gave his hands the power to heal. Charles was actually a bit late in discharging this duty.

Tradition dictated that the king make for Corbigny immediately after having been anointed. But Charles was too busy with his negotiations to follow the dictates of tradition scrupulously.

From Corbigny, the royal party proceeded to Vailly, which had already given the new king its keys, and on to Soissons to accept that town's homage on the twenty-third. At Soissons the king learned that Provins had surrendered to him and decided to make for it. On his way there, he stopped at Château-Thierry on the twenty-ninth and Montmirail on the first of August, to accept their keys.

The real scope of Charles's meandering seems to have been to keep his secret talks alive. On August 2 at Provins, he unexpectedly announced that he had accepted a two-week truce with the Burgundians. The outcome of the truce, he claimed, would be the Anglo-Burgundian surrender of Paris. Joan's response is recorded in a letter to the citizens of Reims:

Jhesus Maria

My dear and good friends, the good and loyal French people of the city of Reims, Joan the Maid sends you her news and begs you and demands that you entertain no doubts about the just quarrel she is pursuing on behalf of the Blood Royal; and I promise you and assure you that I will never abandon you as long as I live and it is true that the King has made a fifteen-day truce with the duke of Burgundy by which he should render him the city of Paris peacefully at the end of a fortnight. However do not be surprised if I do not enter it as quickly; for a truce made in this way is so little to my liking, that I do not know if I shall keep it; but if I keep it, it will only be to safeguard the honor of the king.[6]

But the Anglo-Burgundians had no intention of surrendering Paris without a fight. Their request for a truce, was simply a ruse with which they hoped to gain time. They amassed reinforcements during the truce and even diverted a number of troops which had been levied to fight the crusade, ordered in England by Pope Martin V in 1427 through his legate the cardinal of Winchester, against the heretical Hussites in Bohemians for that purpose. With this move, the English explicitly announced that they considered Joan a heretic. Troops that were levied for a crusade against heretics all made a vow to fight in Christ's name and against his enemies; they constituted a *holy* army. They therefore had to be used in a holy cause. For the English to use them to fight against the Franco-Armagnacs generally, and against Joan specifically, as such, meant that they considered the very war against Joan to be a holy one.

Nor did the Anglo-Burgundians attempt to hide the fact that they wanted a fight. The duke of Bedford, King Henry VI of England's uncle and regent, sent Charles a very insulting challenge just five days after the truce was proclaimed. In it he called Charles everything short of "bastard." He did not spare Joan either. The letter was actually the second official challenge that the English issued after the truce. The first one was an English attempt to engage the French in battle. When Charles's party left Provins, it ran straight into the English, who were already in battle formation. They expected the French to attack, which they did not. Charles responded to the two challenges by attempting to flee. He directed his army to Bray, where he intended to cross the Seine and make for home. He was, however, cut off by the English, who had conquered Bray the day before his planned crossing. Joan and her captains rejoiced. They wanted to fight.

Charles, on the other hand, was determined to respect his truce. He was, at least, consistent on the matter. After his escape had been cut off, he continued to travel from town to town to accept their voluntary surrender. He went to Crépy, Beauvais, La Ferté. The English tried to engage him in battle once again, at Montpilloy on August 14 and 15, where his army ran into the English army in battle formation once again. But no battle ensued then either. After Montpilloy, the English retreated into Paris, clearly baiting the French. Charles's response was to sign yet another truce with the duke of Burgundy, the so-called edict of Compiègne, which he signed on August 28 despite the fact that the duke had not given up the city of Paris after the first truce.

Charles's behavior after his coronation has stunned people for centuries. Some scholars very charitably claim that he simply preferred diplomacy to war, and hence that his continuous parleying was actually his way of attempting to put an end to the war. Some propose that he was simply blinded by guilt when it came to the Philip the Good, the duke of Burgundy. He had, after all, had Philip's father, John the Fearless, killed. His tarrying and negotiating with Burgundy, they therefore suggest, were his attempt to make repairs for his past. Some claim that Charles was simply a dolt who was easily misled, and that the person pulling the strings after Reims was his councilor Georges de la Trémoïlle, who was a well-known Burgundian.

None of these explanations is convincing. In the first place, whatever other things one can say about him, Charles was not a fool. He was certainly fearful. The events ensuing his coronation show as much. He was also moody, which may account for the contradictions to be found in the many descriptions of his character. His contemporaries claimed, for instance, both that he was somber and sober and that he drenched "his passions with drunkenness and debauchery." Still he was not a foolish man. Quite the contrary, he was praised for his intelligence even in his youth.

As for his preferring diplomacy to war, this may very well be true. But Charles knew that there is a time for diplomacy and a time for war. He eventually managed to bring the Hundred Years' War to a close precisely because he understood this. When he finally realized that he could not end the Hundred Years' War without going to the battlefield, he allowed Richemont to return to court and fight his war for him. This took place long after Joan had died.

Perhaps it was Charles's guilt for having had the duke of Burgundy assassinated that blinded him to his own interests during that painful march from Reims. But if that were the case, then it is hard to understand how he ever managed to sign the final treaty with the English in 1453, after he had discovered how badly Joan was treated by her judges in Rouen. Charles found the records of Joan's heresy trial in Rouen when his forces reconquered that town in 1451, and thus two years before the final treaty. It is unlikely that Charles would have felt so much guilt with regard to the death of the duke of Burgandy, but not in regard to Joan's death. For Charles may not have actually ordered the executioner to kill Joan, but he certainly made no move to rescue her or ransom her either.

The reason for Charles's behavior may also have been that he was envious and consciously sacrificing his army and Joan because they made him uncomfortably aware of his own weaknesses. Roman emperors were known to have done such things. The last great Roman general, Aetius, was killed by the assassins of an envious emperor, after he had defeated Attila at the Campi Catalauni. And Charles himself was prone to this sort of thing. "When anyone was lifted high and near to him," claims the Burgundian historian Chastellain, ". . . he began to chafe, and at the first opportunity offered, would cast him down again."[7]

More important than the cause of Charles's blindness, is that his blundering continued, and became more disastrous. After Montpilloy, the king and his army made for Compiègne, which also swore fealty to him. It was August 17. The restless captains of his army, Joan first among them, decided to ride on to Paris. Joan is reported to have said to d'Alençon "my beau duc, get your men and the other captains ready. By my staff, I want to see Paris nearer than I have ever seen it before."[8] Joan later pointed out that it was not on her voices' instruction that she wanted to make for Paris.

The captains waited a week before moving, after which they headed for Senlis, leaving Charles behind to try his hand at the negotiating table once again. Joan, d'Alençon and a small detachment of the army arrived at St. Denis on August 25. They did not have to fight for the town. It had already been deserted by the town's more important inhabitants, who made for Paris when they heard that the attack on Paris was finally to take place. The main body of their army joined them the next day. Joan and d'Alençon then proceeded to attack some of the English strongholds outside of Paris, in preparation for the big battle for the city. Their fighting was successful. Charles, on the other hand, moved on to Senlis two days after Joan and d'Alençon had left for that town. He sent vague promises that he would quickly join his military captains.

On September 1, d'Alençon rode to Senlis in order to convince Charles to make for Paris with the remainder of the army. Time was becoming crucial to the royal army. With every day that passed, Parisian defenses were being fortified. Cannons were being placed, the city's moats were being repaired, pails of rocks, and other things to be thrown at the assailants were being prepared. If the Franco-Armagnac attack was to be successful, it had to take place immediately.

The king told d'Alençon that he would leave for Paris on the following day. But he did not move. So d'Alençon returned to Senlis and the king the next day, when he was told the same thing. Joan's beau duc actually rode back and forth from St. Denis to Senlis each day for about a week, until September 6, when Charles finally kept his word and made for his army in Paris. He arrived in St. Denis on the seventh.

The attack on Paris was staged the next day, which was a mistake. September 8 is a religious holiday—the Nativity of the Virgin—and to the medieval mind, it was blasphemous to wage war on a religious holiday. Joan would pay for this mistake much later. The soldiers' morale was nonetheless high.

Historians have said a number of things about Joan's attack on Paris: that it was generally a mistake; that it was a disaster; that it was the beginning of her military end. Some of these things are true. The battle for Paris was unquestionably the last one in which

Joan led a force as large as the ones she had been accustomed to. It is also unquestionable that Paris marked the end of an era in Joan's life—the era of hope, the hope that Charles would follow her and benefit from what she had to give. Paris also marked the end of Joan's direct communication of her incredible energy, power, and faith to the people of France.

The attack on Paris was not as disastrous as some scholars have said. It was similar to many of those that Joan had led up to that point. The Franco-Armagnac's first assault was against Paris's gate of St. Honoré and was successful. Joan's forces took the gate and burnt the fortifications around it. Joan and her troops then advanced against the gate of St. Denis, which was near the Marché aux Porceaux (the pig market). They filled the moats, crossed them and made for the walls. Initially, it seemed that the attack would be successful, and that all Joan's troops needed to do to get into Paris was to set their scaling ladders and climb them. The Parisian defense was completely thrown at this point.[9] As the Franco-Armagnacs were getting their ladders ready, however, Joan was wounded—an arrow caught her in the thigh. She was carried off the field against her wishes but continued to call out orders. Her orders were in vain; her wound had demoralized her troops and rallied the Parisian defenders. The French withdrew their forces and despite Joan's loud protests, they retreated for the day.

That evening, they set plans for the next day. The details of their plans are not known, but they may have included some sort of a double assault on Paris. D'Alençon ordered that a bridge be built over the Seine in order to cut a new path into the city, and the gate of St. Honoré had already been breached.

There were, naturally, arguments among the captains that evening. A handful of men wished to retreat then and there, and abandon the attempt to conquer the capital of France until a more favorable time. Most of the captains, however, were prepared for a second attack. What is remarkable about the Parisian adventure is that even the dissenting captains agreed to an attack on the following day, when a company of about sixty knights, led by the Sire de Montmorency, rode out of Paris to join Joan and her forces.

There is no way of knowing whether Joan's plans would have led to yet another victory. Charles intervened. On the morning of the next day, Joan rose early, despite her wound, and made for d'Alençon, asking him to sound the attack. He was about to do so, when some couriers arrived from the king with orders for both Joan and d'Alençon. They were to join him at St. Denis immediately. This clearly forced them to postpone the attack. As Joan and d'Alençon were to discover the next morning, however, Charles's intent was more treacherous than they might have supposed. On the morning of September 10, when their army was finally ready to stage its attack on Paris, they found that the king had secretly had d'Alençon's bridge destroyed the night before.[10] Shortly thereafter Charles ordered a complete retreat.

Joan left a suit of armor and a sword in the chapel of St. Denis, after she was ordered to retreat. At her Rouen trial, she claimed that she had done so to thank God for having protected her. "Out of devotion, as is the custom of men-at-arms when they have been wounded; and because she had been wounded before Paris."[10] But there was surely more to her gesture than that. When a soldier hangs up a suit of armor and a sword it is usually because the battle is over. Joan had finally understood that Charles would not allow her to fight. And yet her hope outlived Charles's betrayal of her quest. The suit of armor and sword she hung in the chapel were also the token of her prayer that she be allowed to continue the fight. For she is recorded as having added that, "She offered them to St. Denis, because this was the battle-cry of France."

On September 13, when Charles ordered his army to move on from St. Denis and to return to his own lands, Joan objected. At her Rouen trial she confessed that her voices had told her to stay there and not follow the king. But there was very little Joan could do at that point. She had made a king and had to treat him like one. On September 21, 1429, Charles disbanded the army.

9

The Road to Compiègne

It had to be so, and I was not to be shocked, but accept it.
For God would help me.

—*Joan of Arc*

AFTER THE ROYAL ARMY had been disbanded, Joan no longer had an official role in Charles's court. Nor was there room for her in Charles's plans; they were not military. After his return from Paris, the new king signed yet another treaty with Philip the Good—a four-month armistice, this time—and had every intention of keeping to the diplomatic path. The journey to Reims, which La Trémoïlle had so feared would give Joan ascendancy over him with Charles, had ended up doing precisely the opposite thing: It had made Charles more dependent than ever on La Trémoïlle.

At Gien, where the royal army had been dismissed, d'Alençon asked Charles if Joan might join him in his Beaumont estate. He had put together a small army with which he intended to fight the English in Normandy, and Joan, he claimed, would be very useful in the fight.[1] The request was a reasonable one. By disbanding the army, Charles had, in a sense, fired Joan. There was, as such, no apparent reason for Charles to deny d'Alençon his request. And yet Charles did turn d'Alençon down, upon the suggestion of La Trémoïlle. Joan and d'Alençon were never to see each other, or fight together, again.

D'Alençon wasn't the only person whom Joan was never to see again after the retreat from Paris. In the weeks immediately fol-

Charles VII of France presents a document to Joan. (15th c.) (Courtesy Giraudon/Art

Below: **John the Fearless, duke of Burgandy. Continuing his father's feud, he allied Burgandy with the English claim to rule France, fueling another bitter phase of the Hundred Years' War. He was succeeded by his son Philip the Good.** (Courtesy Alinari/Art Resource, NY)

lowing the retreat, Charles kept Joan at his side and far from her other military friends—Dunois and La Hire. He was probably afraid that she would continue her campaign without him, or his approval, if he lost sight of her. When he left for Bourges from Gien, Joan was therefore with him.

In late September of 1429, Joan was resting in Bourges. She stayed in the house of Marguerite La Touroulde, one of the queen's ladies-in-waiting, at the behest of La Trémoïlle's half brother, Charles d'Albret. She spent three weeks in Marguerite's home, practicing the virtue of patience. She went to mass often; took the sacraments often; and she often asked her hostess to join her at matins—or early morning prayers. She also took the time to give comfort to the poor, as she had done in her childhood. "She was generous with her almsgiving, and most willingly gave to the needy and to the poor, saying that she had been sent for the consolation of the poor and needy."[2]

When she was not on the battlefield, Marguerite claimed, "Joan was innocence itself." She added, however, that ". . . I saw her riding on horseback as the best of soldiers would have done, and the men-at-arms were astonished by it."

Joan's stay at Marguerite's also naturally piqued the curiosity of the good citizens of Bourges, who were eager to see the wonder who had changed the tide of the war. This did not please Joan, to whom patience—and being idolized—must have cost a special effort. Years later, Marguerite was to recall that, "women came to the house while Joan was staying there. They brought rosaries and other objects of piety so that she [Joan] might touch them. This made her laugh and say to me, 'Touch them yourself, they will be as good from your touch as they would be from mine.'"[3]

Simon Beaucroix, one of Joan's companions-at-arms, had a similar recollection of her reaction to adulation. Toward the end of October there was a glimmer of activity. Charles asked Joan to capture 120. Pierre-le-Moûtier and La Charité. The sudden change in Charles's diplomatic course is curious. The most probable reason for it was revenge. In mid-October, Charles discovered just how duped he had been by the duke of Burgundy, for whose sake apparently, he had relinquished all of his military trumps. On the thirteenth of that month, the duke of Bedford, Henry VI of England's uncle and regent, appointed Burgundy lieutenant general of the kingdom of France, and Burgundy accepted the appointment enthusiastically.

As for the specific choice of St. Pierre and La Charité, the towns had been on La Trémoïlle's agenda for quite some time. In June, 1429, and thus many months before Joan was actually commissioned to capture them, he had proposed them as alternative objectives for the royal army, whose captains were determined to proceed to Reims after their crushing victory at Patay. La Trémoïlle had a personal score to settle with Perrinet Gressart, the rather powerful brigand who had conquered the towns in the duke of Burgundy's name in 1423. Gressart had kidnapped the king's councilor in December, 1425, and had forced him to pay a large ransom of fourteen thousand écus—not counting the six thousand he gave in presents to the various members of Gressart's entourage while he was being held in captivity—for his freedom.[4] Yet as eager as both Charles and La Trémoïlle were to exact their revenge, they gave Joan very few men, munitions, and provisions with which to defeat Gressart. This indicates that the king's councilor must still have feared a court coup on Joan's part.

His fear was to be expected. After all, if La Trémoïlle had indeed advised the newly crowned Charles VII of France to abandon the warpath in favor of the diplomatic one, then the reinforcement of the duke of Burgundy's alliance with England must have made the good councilor quite nervous. Philip the Good's becoming the king of England's lieutenant general of France, after his having parleyed with Charles for so long, cannot but have shown the king just how foolish his councilor's advice had been. La Trémoïlle understood this, as he understood that a great accomplishment on Joan's part would put his place at Charles's court at risk. So he forestalled the possibility of a spectacular show. He simply convinced Charles not to give Joan too much in the way of ammunition, men, and provisions. The councilor also sent his brother-in-law, Charles d'Albret, on the Charité campaign to keep a close eye on Joan.

Joan left Bourges with her small army in late October, 1429. With her were d'Albret and Louis de Bourbon. Her siege on St. Pierre was successful. The town fell on November 4. The successful assault was similar to those on Augustins and Le Tourelles. Joan's fellow captains had led an unsuccessful attack on the town and were ready to retreat, when Joan rode up and called for one last assault. That assault won the day. Joan's squire, d'Aulon, recounted how this happened:

> Because of the great number of soldiers in the town and its great strength . . . the French were forced to retire. At that moment I came up. . . . I saw that the Maid had been left with a very small company of her own men and others, and had no doubt she would come to some harm. So I mounted a horse and rushed towards her. I asked her what she was doing alone there like that, and why she had not retreated with the rest. After taking her helmet off her head, she responded that she was not at all alone: that she had 50,000 men in her company, and that she would not leave the spot until she had taken the town.
>
> At that moment, whatever she might have said, she did not have more than four or five men with her. I know this for sure, as do several other men who also saw her. I therefore immediately told her to leave, and retreat as the rest had. She told me to send for sticks and branches to make a bridge over the moat. . . . And when she had said this she shouted 'Sticks and branches, everyone, so that we can make a bridge!' They were brought immediately, and put in place. The entire thing completely astonished me. For the town was immediately taken by assault.[5]

The siege on La Charité, on the other hand, was a dismal affair. Joan and her party set out for the larger town shortly after they had conquered St. Pierre. Rather than making directly north for La Charité, they made south for Moulins. Theirs was a tactical decision. Joan's small army was hopelessly underarmed, understaffed, and underprovisioned, and could not have possibly undertaken the assault in their state.

Once she arrived in Moulins, Joan sent letters to friendly towns asking for help, since Charles had not, and would not send any. The town of Riom responded to Joan's letter by sending her weapons; Clermont-Ferrand responded by sending saltpeter. Orléans, whose gratitude to Joan was of the authentic kind, sent money, clothes, and a gunner.[6] But their help did not suffice. After a very frustrating month, Joan was forced to abandon the attempt to take the town. By then it was December, and a very cold one at that.

After La Charité, Joan made for the royal court. That December, Charles ennobled her and her family, granting them the very rare privilege of making their title inheritable through both the male and female lines.[7] This was, of course, a great honor, which may have been in part prompted by Charles's gratitude. But it was also his courteous farewell to her. By ennobling Joan, Charles granted his kingmaker military freedom; medieval nobility could legally levy armies of their own and wage wars of their own without express permission from the king. (This is the reason why d'Alençon could wage war against the English in Normandy without Charles's support or consent.) Therefore, once Joan was ennobled she no longer had to convince, beg, or force Charles to fight the English, who were still occupying France. She could do so on her own.

But when Charles ennobled Joan and gave her the freedom to wage war on her own, he also made her personally responsible for the wars that she waged with her own troops. And by making Joan the sole responsible party for her own war-waging, he was in essence washing his hands of Joan herself and her quest. By ennobling Joan, Charles made it known that he no longer wanted Joan to fight in his name and that he was no longer interested in her or her quest. Charles's gesture was a courteous but unmistakable farewell.

As of December of 1429, Joan was, essentially on her own. Records indicate that she was in Orléans in January of 1430, and in February she had returned to the king in Bourges. She quickly took advantage of her newly bestowed military freedom. In early March, when she joined the king in Sully La Trémoïlle's castle, she wrote to the citizens of Reims, who were terrified of a Burgundian reprisal for their having sworn allegiance to Charles, promising them that she would personally come to their assistance if they were put under siege. "I will be there," she promised, "and force them [the Anglo-Burgundians] to don their spurs so quickly, that they won't know where they are going." This wasn't the only letter Joan sent from Sully, nor was it the only war which she promised to wage. She also wrote the Hussites, the heretics against whom Pope Martin V had called for a crusade, calling them to return to the Church and threatening them with a crusade of her own if they did not change their ways. The tone of the letter is typical of Joan's ardor, which was as religious as it was French:

> If I don't hear soon that you have mended your ways, that you have returned to the bosom of the Church, I may just leave the English, and turn against you, to eradicate the dreadful superstition with my iron blade and to snatch you from heresy, or from life itself.[8]

At the end of March, she left Sully to do some battling. She headed for Melun, with a small band of men—one hundred and fifty or two hundred soldiers.

It is not clear if she informed Charles of her departure. There is contradictory evidence on the point. However, she no longer needed his consent for her military actions. What is known is that she was joined by captains Piedmontese Bartolomeo Baretta, who had two hundred men; Louis de Bourbon, Regnault of Chartres; a Scottish captain named Kennedy and his men; and several others. Upon her arrival, Melun threw out its Burgundian garrison.

At Melun, Joan's voices told her that she would be captured by the Anglo-Burgundians sometime before the St. Jean, the feast day of John the Baptist, which is June 24. The prospect terrified Joan, who begged her voices to let her die quickly and on the battlefield, rather than in prison after having been captured. But the voices were unrelenting. They told her that, "it must be so, and that she must not be shocked into stupor, but take it in good part, and God would help her." And so Joan went on with her war. A year later, she confessed that she had been able to do so only because her voices had not informed her of the exact day on which she would be captured. No one, she explained, could fight if he knew when exactly he was going to be captured. She did not inform anyone about her imminent capture.

From Melun, Joan left for Lagny, where she captured Franquet d'Arras, a mercenary captain who fought for the Burgundians. Her skirmish against Franquet was actually a close call. Joan pitted her four hundred troops against his three hundred and was very nearly defeated. It took her troops three assaults to defeat their foe, and quite a few men were killed in those assaults. But she was eventually successful. When the skirmish had ended, she took Franquet prisoner and handed him over to the authorities at Senlis on April 24, 1430. The bailiff of Senlis then tried Franquet for his numerous crimes, which included murder, theft, and treachery, among other things. The trial lasted fifteen days, at the end of which Franquet, who confessed that he was guilty of the crimes, was executed. This had actually not been Joan's original intent. Joan had wanted to exchange Franquet for a Franco-Armagnac from Paris, who had recently been arrested for conspiring against the English. The plan went awry because Joan's man had been executed by the English.

At Lagny an extraordinary event took place, which shows the esteem in which the people of France held Joan. After Joan had captured Franquet, several women approached her, and asked her to join them in their prayers for a child who had been stillborn. The child had been dead for three days, and his mother had carried his little body into the abbey-church of St. Pierre and placed it before an image of the Virgin Mary, which was reputed to be miraculous. Her hope was that the child would revive long enough to be baptized and buried in consecrated ground. Medieval faith held that the unbaptized could not go to heaven and could not be buried in consecrated ground.

Joan complied. She followed the women to the church, joined the child's mother, and "prayed and finally life appeared in the child which yawned three times and was then baptized. Then it died, and was buried in consecrated ground." News of the miracle spread far and quickly. During her Rouen trial, which took place a year after the child was resuscitated, Joan herself was asked to comment on the event.[9]

Joan appeared next in Compiègne on May 14, where the Anglo-Burgundians were preparing a major offensive. Philip of Burgundy had arrived at Noyen, just fifteen miles north of the town on May 6, and was working toward Compiègne. He was to join a large English force led by the earl of Arundel and lay siege to the town, which remained obstinately loyal to the oath of fealty it had sworn to Charles after his coronation. Joan hurried to the town as soon as she heard that it was in peril.

There was nothing much that Joan could do with her four hundred men against the much greater forces of her foes. But on May 14, she tried to cut off Burgundy's advance by staging a surprise attack on Pont-l'Evéque, a town which was some five miles north of Compiègne, where there was a bridge spanning the Oise. Joan knew that Burgundy would have to cross that bridge to reach Compiègne. Her attack was initially successful, and would have been completely so, had the Burgundians guarding the bridge not received reinforcements.

Joan tried to stage another surprise attack on Choisy two days later. Her plan was to circle around the town of Choisy and attack the English troops garrisoned there from behind. To circle around the English troops, however, Joan needed to ride her small force through Soissons, and Soissons would not let her band of men pass through its gates. After having reneged its Anglo-Burgundian allegiance and sworn fealty to Charles in his triumphant post-coronation march, the town had turned coats once again.

Joan moved on to Crépy, where she learned that the earl of Arundel had arrived at Compiègne. Upon hearing the news, she immediately left for Compiègne, despite her troops' protests. It was too risky, they claimed. To which Joan retorted, "By my staff, we are enough. I will go to see my good friends at Compiègne."[10] She entered its gates safely on the morning of May 23. That in itself was a feat. The town was almost completely surrounded by enemy troops when Joan made for it.

That afternoon she led one last surprise attack against the Burgundian camp at Margny, which was directly north of Compiègne, and threatened its gate of Notre Dame. Her attack on the camp was successful. The Burgundians there were routed. As they were desperately trying to reassemble, however, Jean de Luxembourg, who just happened to be doing some surveying in the vicinity of the camp, heard that a battle was taking place, sounded the alarm and quickly rode to the camp's aide. He arrived in time to force Joan's troops back toward Compiègne's gate of Notre Dame, which had a bridge in front of it.

At her Rouen trial, Joan recounted that she managed to fight the reinforcements back from the gate and bridge twice. The third time she tried to do so, her own troops began to retreat towards the gate. New reinforcements had arrived; the English, too, had heard the alarm. There was nothing Joan could do to stop her men from pulling back once the English arrived So she and a small handful of her very loyal men turned to cover their comrades' retreat. Joan managed to beat the Anglo-Burgundian troops away from the bridge and gate a third time, when Compiègne closed the outer portcullis of the gate at her back. That was the end. Joan was quickly surrounded by her enemies, pulled off her horse, and taken prisoner.[11] It was May 23, 1430.

10

Beaurevoir

It is a prisoner's right to escape.

—*Joan of Arc*

JOAN WAS TO LIVE for a whole year after she was captured. She spent that entire year in prison. It was brought to a close on the stake. From the time of her capture till roughly mid-June, 1430, she was held in Jean de Luxembourg's castle of Beaulieu. She was then transferred to Luxembourg's castle of Beaurevoir, where she was held until November. In December of that same year, she was handed over to the English, who had paid her large ransom, and quickly sent her to Rouen. In Rouen she was tried for heresy by a very large inquisition, composed mostly of professors of the University of Paris. Her trial officially began in January, 1431, and lasted till May, of that same year. She was executed on May 30, 1431.

After the portcullis of Compiègne's gate of Notre Dame had been lowered, Joan and those very few loyal companions of hers who formed the rearguard which protected her forces' retreat— her squire d'Aulon, her brother Pierre, Poton de Xaintrailles, who had fought with her since Orléans, and a few others—were left to defend themselves. It was a hopeless situation. The English and the Burgundians had rushed en masse to the northern gate of Compiègne once they heard the alarm sounded by Jean de Luxembourg.

While the events of Joan's life are difficult to interpret, they are well documented. *Above:* After the siege of Orléans was raised, the clerk entered the event in the register of the Paris Parliament. His sketch in the margin is the earliest extant image of Joan. (Courtesy Giraudon/Art Resource, NY) *Right:* Copy of a painting of Joan in the Glory of Saint Peter in Rome. (Courtesy Snark/Art Resource, NY)

Joan was riding a charger at the time and was wearing a spectacular scarlet and gold *huque* over her armor. She always made herself visible during a fray, so that her troops could locate her in an instant, and know where to go for orders, courage, and whatever else they might need. Once her small band of men had been surrounded, a man named Lyonnel rushed to her, grabbed the long panels of her surcoat, and pulled her off her horse. Lyonnel was an archer, who served in an Anglo-Burgundian company under the captaincy of Jean de Wandomme. After a few minutes of real surprise on her captors' part (they could not believe that they had actually captured the Pucelle d'Orléans), Lyonnel handed Joan over to Wandomme.

Wandomme, who was best known as the "Bastard of Wandomme," was one of Jean de Luxembourg's vassals. What this meant was that Joan was officially Luxembourg's, and not Wandomme's, prisoner. In the Middle Ages, war prizes, as great as Joan was, were to be handed to one's feudal overlord. Luxembourg was the count of Ligny, and a staunch Anglo-Burgundian. Not only was the duke of Burgundy technically his suzerain, he also had his own direct contacts with the English, and he received a monthly pension of 500 livres from the English crown.[1] Joan had, as such, indirectly fallen into the hands of both of her archenemies: the Burgundians and the English.

None of this put Joan's life in any immediate danger. Unlike modern military etiquette, medieval etiquette had it that prisoners of war, the important ones that is, were held for ransom and would be given their freedom once their ransoms were paid. And Joan was a very important prisoner of war. The Anglo-Burgundians rejoiced mightily at her capture. For they feared her as they "feared no captain or leader."[2] Her ransom shows as much. It was set at 10,000 écus.

Once Jean de Luxembourg received his prisoner of war, he was immediately presented with a problem: What was he to do with her? There were many people who were eager to get their hands on Joan. The duke of Bedford, who represented the English crown, was one of them. Joan had been a major stumbling block in his French campaign. She had reversed the winds of what had seemed to him to be an easy victory of the long war for the French throne. Her troops had defeated his soldiers, terrified them, and slaughtered them.

Bedford also had a very definite opinion about Joan, which he expressed in a letter to Charles after Joan's victory at Orléans, saying, "You are aided and abetted most of all by superstitious and depraved individuals, by that disorderly and deformed travesty of a woman, who dresses like a man."[3] Bedford was a conservative man. He had a precise image of what religion should be, and figures like Joan, who abetted people to rebel against the political status quo in God's name, played no part in it. This is not too terribly surprising. In the late fourteenth century, England had had a difficult time with demagogues who called people to rebel against the state in the name of religion. There was, for instance, a large uprising of English peasants in 1381—which had quickly turned into a religious movement called Lollardy—that was as opposed to the institutionalized Church as it was to the politics of its day.[4] Revolts like these posed an enormous threat to medieval political institutions not only because they openly attacked them but more importantly because they attacked their foundations. Medieval politics had religious foundations: The king was so by divine right. Thus, to attack the institutionalized Church was to endanger the entire medieval political structure.

Bedford understood this. Hence Joan, who fit what Bedford considered the role of the religious demagogue, was, in his view, most clearly a scourge to be stamped out. That she had fought in the name of both the monarchy—Charles of Valois—and the religious foundation of the monarchy (it was God, she claimed, who had given her the quest to restore the "Blood Royal") made no difference to him. For she had fought on the wrong side.

The professors of the University of Paris were also eager to seize Joan; they had been for at least a year and a half. In November of 1429, the University had written the pope accusing Joan of heresy, since she "pretended to know and say things that are to come."[5] Joan was a threat to the University. By the fifteenth century, the University of Paris had become an arrogant institution, which more or less considered itself the principal defender of the faith. It was therefore very suspicious of any outsider who said or did anything in God's name without consulting its illustrious faculty. The roots of the University of Paris's arrogance were many. It had long been one of the main centers of intellectual activity in Europe and many of its professors—Alexander of Hales, Thomas Aquinas, Bonaventure, Albert the Great, to name a few—had become doctors of the Church. The University was justly proud of its tradition, and used it to back its own opinion of itself. Furthermore, the University considered itself to be one of the very few unchanging institutions amidst the great religious turmoil of the late fourteenth and early fifteenth century, when the coexistence of popes and anti-popes had become commonplace. It therefore felt that it stood above the disorders of its day, and could issue judgements on them.

The University of Paris also felt threatened by Joan's position on the matter of the kingship of France: it was in direct opposition to the University's own. After the Treaty of Troyes, the University had backed the English takeover of the throne of France in God's name. The arguments they proposed in its favor intended to demonstrate that it was God's own will that the kingdoms of France and England be united. After all, they argued, since the division of the two kingdoms had led to war, sedition, and the diminution of faith, their union would bring about the immediate cessation of hostilities and usher in a new age of hope.[6] The argument was a logical and reasonable one and held the weight of a sentence issued by a higher court. Joan, as far as the University was concerned, had to be a fraud.

Joan's Ransom

What was behind Luxembourg's reticence? Why did the count make his own allies wait six months before allowing them to pay Joan's ransom? What is certain is that it was not money that kept Luxembourg from giving Joan to the Anglo-Burgundians. Cauchon had offered the price of 10,000 écus (which was the amount he eventually paid for her) at the very beginning of his negotiations with Luxembourg. No one proposed a counteroffer in the interim.

It may have been sympathy for Joan that kept Luxembourg from turning her over to Cauchon. Luxembourg may have liked Joan personally, and have honestly attempted to help her avoid what he must have known would be her end if he allowed Cauchon to pay her ransom. It was widely known or understood that the English would have her condemned for heresy and burnt at the stake. Their plans were already overt in August 1429, when they diverted troops meant to fight against the Hussites to fight against Charles's army. For those troops had vowed to fight against heretics. That they were used to fight against Joan, therefore, shows that the English were ready to use the heretic card at that point.[7]

Had Luxembourg's reticence indeed been dictated by pity or sympathy for Joan, this might explain the strange visit he paid her in her prison cell in Rouen. Long after he had sold her to the English, Luxembourg called on Joan and offered to pay her ransom if she promised never to fight again. Joan laughed at his offer. She lucidly pointed out that the English would never give her up, because they wanted her dead. She thus deduced that he was taunting her, by proposing to buy her back. Luxembourg, however, replied that his offer was serious. Yet there are not records of his attempting to ensure here release.

His reticence may, on the other hand, also have been caused by fear. Luxembourg may have honestly been afraid of being an accomplice to Joan's death; perhaps he took her claim to be have been sent by God seriously. The cause of Luxembourg's reticence may also have been the women in his life: his wife, aunt, and stepdaughter, Jeanne de Béthune, Jeanne de Luxembourg, and Jeanne de Bar. All three women were Armagnac, and all three liked Joan, whom they had come to know quite well while she was held in the castle of Beaurevoir. This was especially true of Jeanne of Luxembourg. It may be that these women, none of whom wanted to see Joan in English hands, put inordinate pressure on Jean to keep him from accepting Cauchon's offer.

It is, however, also possible that Luxembourg was an honorable man, who felt it best to respect his times' mores, and to give his own enemy—Charles of Valois—the chance to pay his prisoner's ransom.[8]

These two parties, who longed to gain possession of Joan, were not independent entities. The University had long been an ally of the English crown. The two institutions were, as such, perfectly willing to combine their efforts to ensure that Joan was given to them. Their joint efforts were mediated by Pierre Cauchon, the Bishop of Beavais. He was a zealous man who had a personal score to settle with Joan. A devout Burgundian, he had been ousted from his city when it swore allegiance to Charles on his triumphal post-coronation march and was replaced by a bishop Charles had appointed.

Luxembourg's loyalty to the Anglo-Burgundian cause should have prompted him to immediately accept Cauchon's offer to pay Joan's ransom, and hand her over to his care. And yet, Luxembourg was not intent on selling Joan to the Anglo-Burgundians. He not only turned down their first two offers to pay her ransom—the first made on May 26, 1430, and thus just three days after Joan's capture, and the second made in July—he made the Anglo-Burgundian spokesman wait six long months before agreeing to sell him Joan.

It seems beyond doubt, that the point behind Luxembourg's making Cauchon wait six months before allowing him to buy Joan, was to secure Joan some buyer other than Cauchon. But the Armagnacs, King Charles VII to be precise, made no offer to pay Joan's ransom, despite the fact that many people urged him to do so. One of the people who entreated Charles to pay Joan's ransom was Jacques Gelu, the archbishop of Embrun, who wrote the king a very strong letter on the matter.[9] The greatest request for intervention on Charles's part came from the people of France, who had been praying for Joan's release since her capture at Compiègne. Candles were lit on her behalf; masses were said; public processions undertaken. In the procession at Tours, all of the Cathedral clergy walked barefoot through the streets praying for her.[10] One of the prayers to be said at a mass offered for Joan's safety at Grenoble was:

Almighty and Everlasting God, Who in Thine holy and ineffable clemency and in Thine admirable power hast ordained the coming of a young girl for the glory and preservation of the realm of France and also to repel, confound and destroy the enemies of the kingdom, and Who has allowed that when she had devoted herself to the holy tasks by Thee commanded, she should be imprisoned by the enemy, grant us, we implore Thee, through the intercession of the Blessed Ever-Virgin Mary and all the Saints, that she may be delivered from the power unharmed, and that she may accomplish all that Thou has prescribed by one and the same mission.[11]

But Charles did nothing for Joan, which is, of course, very strange. For he did pay at least a part of La Hire's ransom when he was captured a year or so later.

Charles's silence put Jean de Luxembourg in an awkward position. With no Armagnac counteroffer, he was virtually forced to sell Joan to the English. Philip of Burgundy was his liege lord after all, and Luxembourg was on the English payroll. He could not continue to turn the English down for no reason other than his honor, fear, or sympathy.

When Joan got wind of the fact that Luxembourg was about to hand her over to Cauchon, she attempted to escape. She was said to have leapt off the seventy-foot tower of the Castle of Beaurevoir where she was being held prisoner, or at least that is how her Rouen judges interpreted the attempted escape.[12] More likely she attempted to climb off the tower and slipped. This was at least her second attempt to escape; she had made the first while she was being held in Beaulieu. Neither one was successful; neither one averted what had become her fate. Joan was sold to Cauchon on November, 21, 1430.

11

Rouen: Preamble to the End

Grant that she may accomplish all that Thou hast prescribed
by one and the same mission
—popular prayer for Joan while she was being held captive

AFTER CAUCHON HAD MANAGED to settle the matter of Joan's ransom, which was funded by the purse of the English crown,[1] he had her transferred to Rouen, where she spent the last five months of her life held captive by the English. Indeed, the very reason why she had been sent to Rouen in the first place, rather than to Paris where the University had wanted to hold her trial was that "the king of England and his principal counselors were then in Rouen."[2]

Joan was imprisoned in a small cell in the tower of the castle at Rouen, which has since been called the Tour de la Pucelle. She was put in leg irons and chained by the waist to a large block of wood while she was in her cell. An iron cage had also been constructed for her. It is not altogether certain that the cage was ever used, which is to say that no witnesses reported having seen Joan in it. It was nonetheless there for a purpose, just as the chains and irons were. Joan's jailers were not going to take any chances with her; they knew she would attempt to escape; they did not know what means she would use to do so.

The English had handpicked an entire company of soldiers to guard Joan. The company was captained by a man named John Grey. There were at least five guards in her cell with her at all

Above: **Joan imprisoned in Rouen castle, where she was held, after being sold to the English, tried and condemned.** (Courtesy Giraudon/Art Resource, NY) *Below:* **From a 15th c. anonymous manuscript, Trial of Joan of Arc.** (Courtesy Giraudon/Art Resource, NY)

times. Her jailers even slept in her cell, making sleeping a dangerous thing for her. As she was to point out to Cauchon and the earl of Warwick, "I do not dare to take off these leggings, or wear them if they are not tightly laced. You both know that my jailers have tried to do violence to me several times. Once, while I cried out, you came to help me; had you not come, I should have been the victim of my guards."[3] During the day they taunted her, bullied her, and assaulted her. They even put her on public display. Jean de Luxembourg wasn't Joan's only visitor while she was in prison; people of all kinds came to catch a glimpse of her.

All of this was most irregular. The Church had its own jails and jailers for heretics, and these were certainly not of the sort in which Joan was held. The strong military surveillance is, however, important because it is a very good indication of the nature and importance of Joan's trial.

Many things have been said about Joan's Rouen trial: that it was unfair; that it was illegal; that it was political rather than religious; that it was extremely biased; that it was brutal. All of these things are true. But they do not really capture the essence of Joan's case, which is that the English authorities had taken Joan more seriously than the French authorities had. The English had understood the nature of Joan's quest more so than the French had. They had also grasped its implications more so than the French had, and had attempted to come to terms with those implications as the French had not.

One of the abiding questions behind Joan's story is if Charles of Valois and his councilors had ever really believed Joan's claim that she had been sent by God to free France, or understood the weight of that claim. They certainly behaved as though they hadn't. After Joan had been captured, Regnault of Chartres, the archbishop of Reims, who had been on Joan's glorious march toward Reims, denounced Joan and attempted to replace her with another visionary. This other visionary, he claimed—whose name is recorded as Guillaume the Shepherd—would be just as effective as Joan had been in defeating the English.[4] The fact that Guillaume never delivered what Regnault had promised was perhaps to be expected. What is astonishing is that the archbishop thought that Joan could be so easily replaced, and that other high-ranking members of Charles's court were of like mind. This would seem to indicate that Charles's court had never really taken Joan, or her quest, seriously.

The irony is that both the duke of Bedford and Pierre Cauchon not only took Joan very seriously, but also seem to have fully understood the implications of her quest. Just how much they did can be seen in the difference in the ways in which they dealt with Joan and with the poor shepherd Guillaume after they had captured them. When the English finally gained possession of Joan, they staged an enormous trial in order to disprove her claim to have been sent by God to liberate France. They disbursed an enormous amount of money for the trial and did not have Joan executed until the court had officially excommunicated her. Guillaume, on the other hand, they dispatched much less ceremoniously. On December 16, 1431, when they decided to have the young Henry VI of England crowned king of France in order to reinstate his claim to the French throne, Guillaume was a key feature in their coronation procession. They dragged him in chains through the city of Paris to show just how empty their enemy's claim that God was opposed to their annexation of France had been. After the procession, they put the shackled Guillaume in a sack and threw him in the Seine.[5] They did not feel that it was necessary to prove that he had not been sent by God.

What was it that the English authorities had understood, and the French had not? The answer lies in the nature of Joan's quest—in her claim that God had sent her to free France of the English. There is something absurd about that quest, both because it implies that God is not a pacifist, and because it implies that France is a sacred nation. Both implications are startling. God's sending Joan to battle did not sound as striking to the medieval mind, as it does today. To the modern mind, the very idea that God can want people to wage war sounds contradictory. After all, it was God who the commanded "Thou shalt not kill." And war necessarily entails killing. God said that *the meek shall inherit the Earth*. And waging war is quite the contrary of being meek. And it was God who said to *render unto Caesar what is Caesar's*. And God's intervening in Caesar's war seems to contradict that distinction. The modern mind therefore dismisses the idea altogether. Theologians and metaphysicians both teach that God cannot contradict himself. A priori, as such, Joan's quest is looked at as something dubious. This is why so many modern scholars have attempted to find ways of dismissing Joan's claim.

The medieval mind, on the other hand, had no difficulty with the idea of a holy war per se, or with the notion that war could be a holy thing. Martyrs and saints of all kinds were often viewed as warriors, even if they did not engage in physical battles. For saints and martyrs engaged in battle with the enemy of all enemies—the tempter, the snake of the Garden of Eden, the fallen angel—and martyrs and saints were holy people.

Nor did the medieval mind have a problem with thinking of a physical war as a holy quest. Peter the Hermit called medieval kings to send armies to the Holy Lands—to launch the first crusade—and got the support of one of the holiest men of the day—Bernard of Clairvaux. Peter was just the first of many men who called for a holy war. The idea stuck once it was formulated, and took on many different forms. There were crusades against infidels and crusades against heretics. Adults went on crusades and so did children. Crusading continued up to Joan's day. Joan herself wanted to go on one, as she claimed in her letter to the Hussites.[6]

What the medieval mind did have a problem with, however, was conceiving of a war among Christians, who were loyal to the pope, as a holy war. This is not to say that medieval Catholics never waged war on each other. Good Christian kings even fought the pope in the Middle Ages, and some popes fought back. It is to say that war among Christians (who were loyal to the pope) was not viewed as a *holy* war. It belonged to a different category. In other words, the medieval mind found it difficult to conceive of a war among Christians as the kind of war that God himself might inspire.

As such, when Joan claimed that God had called her to free France of the English, her claim sounded preposterous. Indeed, to some it sounded like an abomination. Charles had understood this much, at least. It is why he had had Joan extensively examined by a court of theologians before giving her an army. He needed official Church approval in order to allow Joan to fulfill her quest. What Charles had not understood, however, was that if Joan had indeed been sent by God, then the war she called him to fight, the war for the throne of France, was a holy war. And what this meant was not only that he could not lose it, but also that it was sinful for him not to fight it.

Who had understood this, ironically enough, were the English authorities. The English knew that if God had indeed sent Joan to free France, they would not only suffer an incredible loss of temporal power (their lands in France as well as the French throne, which the Treaty of Troyes had made theirs), but that they would also suffer in the hereafter. For if God wanted France to belong to the French king, then their attempt to seize the French throne was not only doomed, it was also sinful, and put their eternal souls in peril. Therefore, they had to do everything in their power to prove that Joan was not a holy quester. They had to try with all of their might to dispel the very notion that God could have wanted France to win the war. This is why they staged an Inquisition, an official Church trial to deal with Joan. For it was only the Church that could determine whether Joan's claim was authentic or not.

As fearful as they may have been for their souls, however, the English did not go through with a fair Inquisition. Had they wanted a fair hearing on Joan's case, they would have gone to Rome, where Pope Martin V may just have given Joan his blessing. The pope had already let the English know that he was seriously displeased at their having used the crusaders, levied for the war against the Hussites, to fight against Joan.[7] As frightened as the English were for their souls, they put the matter of Joan's Inquisition in hands that would ensure an outcome which was favorable to them. This is the reason why they let one of their most devoted pawns, Pierre Cauchon, direct the ecclesiastical proceedings. The English needed Joan to be wrong. Cauchon had a considerable reputation. Not only was he the archbishop of Beauvais—at least as far as the English were concerned—and hence a high-ranking member of the Church, he was also a scholar: He had been the rector of the University of Paris. He was also a well-tried English partisan.

Cauchon, too, understood what was at stake in Joan's case. He knew that if Joan was an authentic prophet, he was doomed for having chosen the wrong side in the war. Therefore he had to use every means at his disposition to have Joan discredited and eliminated. This is why he made Joan's condemnation as a heretic, her excommunication, and her death at the stake *his* quest. This is what was at stake at Joan's Rouen trial. It is what makes the end of Joan's life such an incredible clash of wills.

Proceedings began on January 9, 1431. They ended on May 30 of that same year, when Joan was burnt at the stake. There were three different phases to the trial. The first was a sort of interrogation, during which the court defined the charges against Joan. This phase lasted from January 9 to March 26. The second phase was the actual trial, which ended with Joan's abjuration. It lasted from March 26 to May 24. The third phase was actually a second hearing, in which Joan was tried for having relapsed. It was very brief. It began on May 28 and ended a day later.

Joan of Arc by Eugene Grasset (19th c.). Joan's martyrdom provided a traditional framework for the concept of heroic virtue.
(Courtesy Victoria & Albert Museum, London/Art Resource, NY)

12

Rouen: The Trial

I have done nothing which was not commanded by God.
—*Joan of Arc*

CAUCHON HAD PROMISED the English a *pulchrum processum*, a beautiful trial.[1] He was confident that the trial would be an easy one. The one-time Chancellor of the University had packed his court with Parisian academics and was convinced that they would make short work of Joan, who was unschooled, illiterate, and a woman. He was quickly proven wrong. Cauchon's first problems arose before the hearings had begun. His handpicked court quickly let him know that it was not as eager as he was to put Joan on trial.

In early February, Cauchon's would-be right-hand man, Jean Le Maître, the trial's Vice Inquisitor, decided that he wanted nothing to do with the proceedings. "He refused to take part several times, and did everything he could not to become mixed up with it."[2] Cauchon had to force Le Maître to take his post. "Some people he [Le Maître] knew told him that if he persisted in his absence, he would be in danger of death. In fact, he only made up his mind under pressure from the English. I often heard him say to me, 'I see that if this matter is not dealt with as the English want, my life is over.'"[3]

Le Maître was not the only prospective member of the court who refused to take part in the trial. The most vociferous was Nicolas de

Houppeville, a priest from the diocese of Rouen, who pointed out that there were several reasons why the trial was gravely flawed. The most important was that Joan had already received the Church's sanction. The hearing at Poitiers, led by the archbishop of Reims, had declared her a good Catholic. Cauchon's response was to have the priest reprimanded, and imprisoned.

As Cauchon was soon to discover, however, an edgy set of judges and assessors was the least of his problems. The first phase of his proceedings against Joan began with a huge fiasco. Once he had paid Joan's ransom, Cauchon had sent people to the towns where Joan was well known to try to uncover unsavory information about her. He needed some crime with which to accuse her in order to begin his trial. Inquisitorial trials were supposed to be based on a *diffamatio*—charges which were well established—before the trial began. But his runners came back empty handed. Nothing even vaguely suspicious, from the religious point of view, had been reported about Joan.

The fact that Cauchon had no diffamatio meant that he would have to interrogate Joan in order to establish charges against her. That prospect was not a pleasing one. It meant that he would not have a solid case against Joan, unless she confessed to some grave crime. More importantly, it made the proceedings highly irregular from a legal point of view. It was virtually unheard of for a heresy trial to be based "exclusively on the interrogation of the accused without anyone, including the accused herself, knowing what charge was being brought against her."[4]

Cauchon's first objective was, therefore, to find charges that would stick to Joan and, which would make her claim to have been sent by God to liberate France sound heretical or false. Cauchon's mission was to find some way of insinuating that Joan's quest was not divinely inspired, that her mystical experiences, her conversations with her voices, were not authentic—that God did not communicate his will directly to Joan. It was on the divine origin of the mission that the matter of the innocence or culpability of the English rested.

Despite the rocky beginning of his trial, Cauchon was confident. He had promised the English a *pulchrum processum*, a beautiful trial, and he intended to give them one. And he had every reason to be confident. To make the extraordinary claim that heavenly voices are the cause of one's actions sound suspicious, or false, is
not that terribly difficult. All Cauchon needed to do was show that
those very actions, which Joan claimed to have been inspired by
heaven, were actually caused by something else altogether. Or he
could also establish that the voices which Joan heard were not
heavenly. And these are precisely the things Cauchon intended to
do. In his initial line of questioning, Cauchon concentrated on two
things. The first was whether Joan's war-waging was indeed dictated by "voices," or whether it had some other motivation: local
patriotism, implicit or explicit homosexuality on Joan's part. The
second was whether Joan's "voices" were caused by something
other than divine intervention. In this latter line of questions, he
narrowed the possible causes of Joan's hearing voices down to
three: a physical disorder, a mental disorder, and witchcraft.

The court held six public sessions in which it called upon Joan
to answer questions on matters related to her mission. The sessions took place between February 21 and March 3, 1431. In them
the court asked Joan to describe how she experienced her voices
and when she began to do so. It asked her about her eating habits
and whether she had physical contact with her voices. It asked her
if she desired to be a man. It asked her to describe her relations to
her family, her childhood, and about Domrémy's politics and customs. Questions then shifted to her reasons for attacking Paris on
a feast day, and on to witchcraft, to a miracle Joan was reported to
have performed in Lagny, and to the physical appearance of her
voices. All of these questions were fired in rapid succession, and
without any apparent order, in hopes of extorting a confession out
of Joan. The court also used the surprise change-of-subject tactic,
jumping from an apparently innocent question like, "Did you take
communion often?" to a question such as, "Why did you steal the

The Phenomenon of Joan's Voices

Cauchon's approach to the matter of Joan's voices is surprisingly modern. The scores of scholars, who have picked up his torch and tried to give a naturalistic explanation to the phenomenon of Joan's voices, have all followed one of the routes which he outlined at the trial. Physicians have given their input and called upon all types of physical disorders in order to prove that something other than God was the cause of Joan's visions and behavior. Some claim that Joan's visions are actually the proof that she had Ménière's disease. The disease, after all, produces many odd visual and auditory disturbances. Others claim that she had a genetic disorder—that her chromosomes were not female—in order to explain her belligerence.

There are psychologists who claim that Joan's visions were actually wish-fulfilling dreams.[5] Joan was, they point out, an adolescent when she began to hear her voices, and adolescents are prone to have strange experiences. Others state that her crossdressing was a sign of her desire to be a man.[6] Others yet call upon latent homosexuality to explain her behavior.[7] Those that do so are naturally at odds with those colleagues of theirs who claim that Joan's visions were the wish-fulfilling fantasies of a pubescent girl. For the latter group naturally presupposes that Joan's tendencies were heterosexual—Joan's first voice being St. Michael's.

Anthropologists and feminists have also entered the fray, proposing many of what Karen Sullivan calls "spiritualist" interpretations of Joan's mystical experiences. They claim that Joan was involved in the occult, and that it is witchcraft that explains her strange power.[8] These spiritualist interpreters attempt to back their claim through Joan's own testimony. When pressured by the Inquisitors, Joan stated that she had experienced her voices near the fountain by the *arbre des fées*—-the fairy tree—in the vicinity of Domrémy. Her brother, on the other hand, claimed that Joan had had her first mystical experience in the *Bois Chesnu*, the oak grove near her home.[9] Oak groves were sacred to the Celts, and one of the characteristics of Celtic religion, was its belief in sprites and fairies. Were Joan's voices, they ask, not the fruit of some sort of revival of pagan rites?

bishop of Senlis's horse?" and on to a more serious and relevant one such as, "How old was the baby in Lagny?"

As optimistic as Cauchon may have been at the beginning of the trial, it did not take the Inquisitor long to realize that Joan would make the proceedings extremely difficult for him. She gave him a good sample of her extraordinary intelligence at the very onslaught of her first interrogation, when no amount of pressure on his part could get Joan to take an oath to tell the truth, the *whole* truth, and nothing but the truth. When Joan was asked to swear, she replied, "I do not know what you will ask me. There may be some questions to which I will not respond." Cauchon retorted that the questions that she would be asked would all have to do with matters of faith. To which Joan's responded:

I will willingly swear to respond to questions regarding my father, my mother, and what I have done since I have come to France. But as for matters regarding the revelations I have had from God, I have only told Charles, my king, about them. And even if you were to cut off my head, I would not tell you a single word about them, because my voices have forbidden me to.[10]

Cauchon then rejoined, "Will you swear to respond truthfully to questions regarding our faith?" Joan ended up swearing to tell the truth on matters concerning the faith, and only on those.

And that was just the beginning. Joan quickly let the court know that she had no intention of succumbing to its pressure tactics. She refused to recite *Our Father*, until she was allowed to confess before a priest. She refused to swear that she would not attempt to escape. Prisoners, she stated, "Have the right to escape," and protested loudly about the chains and irons which she was forced to wear. The court was stunned. Such was the clamor in the courtroom on the first day of the proceedings that the notaries complained that they could not do their job if order was not brought to the courtroom:

When the first questions were put to Joan, a great tumult arose. Joan was interrupted at every word, when she spoke of her visions; and there were two or three secretaries of the English king who took down her declarations according to their own fancy, omitting her excuses and everything that could have brought to her exoneration. I complained and said that if things did not become more orderly, I would not accept the responsibility of holding the pen.[11]

Joan was not just a recalcitrant witness, she was a very difficult one to pin down. She was brash, funny, and fully aware of what Cauchon was attempting to do. Régine Pernoud, the great late medieval historian, points out that after the first few days of interrogation, the minutes, which recorded Joan's responses, began to report these in the third person, in order to tone down the strength of Joan's responses. This gives a very good idea of the discomfort that Joan's persuasiveness must have caused in the courtroom.

Cauchon's discomfort must have been exceptional. Joan quickly punched holes into his carefully laid line of questioning. Try as he might to force Joan to give him some evidence that would allow him to suggest that her voices were not the direct cause of her waging war on the Anglo-Burgundians, Joan would not concede the point. On the morning of February 22, 1431, while she was being sworn in for her second interrogation she warned him: "If you were better informed about me, I'm sure you would have never wanted for me to fall in your hands! I have done nothing, if not on revelation." Two days later during her third interrogation she warned Cauchon to be careful with his judgements, because he was putting himself in grave danger:

Be careful, you who call yourself my judge! Be careful about what you are doing. Because my quest does come from God, and you are taking a terrible risk!

In the fourth interrogation she stated that she would rather have been "cut into pieces, than have come to France without God's support."[12]

Nor was Cauchon any more successful in getting Joan to contradict herself on the matter. Try as his court might to suggest that it was Joan's hometown's patriotism, rather than her voices that made her go to war, she simply would not concede the point. She was willing to admit that Domrémy was staunchly Armagnac, and that the children of Domrémy had fistfights with the children from the nearby Burgundian village of Maxey. But when the court asked whether she had decided to take up the fight against the Anglo-Burgundians when she was very young, and at her village's behest, she replied that her allegiance to the king stemmed from her voices' own urging. "When I understood that my voices were for the king of France, I began to hate the Burgundians." The most Joan would concede on the matter of her having been sent by God to liberate France, was that she had participated in some battles which her voices had not specifically commanded her to fight: those of Paris and La Charité.

Since Joan would not relent on the matter of her having gone to war on her voices' instruction, Cauchon was left with his second tactic: to try to get her to admit that her voices were not divinely inspired. He insinuated that Joan dabbled in magic, apparently hoping that she would slip and admit something that would allow his court to infer that she did. He and his colleagues therefore not only asked Joan innumerable questions regarding the lingering echoes of pagan rites in Domrémy's local customs, they also wanted to know whether she had invoked her voices in any way. If, in other words, she had power over them and if she treated any part of her armor or jewelry as though it were an amulet of sorts.

There was, for instance, in the vicinity of Domémy a large beech tree, the so-called "Ladies' Tree" or "Fairy Tree," on which young girls were wont to hang garlands in the spring. This tree was said to have a miraculous fountain next to it, and old women whispered that one could see the fairies there. The Inquisitor thus asked Joan sev-

17

eral times about the tree's significance, whether she had ever seen fairies. He also asked her where she had hidden her mandrake root.

Joan's answers to these various questions were always clear and succinct. "The Ladies' Tree," she stated:

> is large . . . At times I went there with other girls to make garlands to adorn the statue of Our Lady in Domrémy with its leaves. Old people . . . used to say that fairies gathered next to the tree to talk. I heard Jeanne Aubry, the wife of the mayor and my godmother, tell me that she had seen fairies there. I do not know if this is true. I have never seen a fairy near the tree, as far as I know. And if I saw them elsewhere, I certainly do not know about it! I saw some girls from my village put garlands of flowers on its branches, and at times I did so myself. . . . But when I came to know that I was to come to France, I spent little time in games and play. As little as possible. I don't know if I danced around the tree, once I reached the age of reason; I may have done so with other girls; maybe I played more than I danced . . . I heard my brother tell what the people of Domrémy were saying, which is this: "Joan was given her mission near the Fairy Tree." This is false.[13]

As for mandrake roots, Joan told the Inquisition that she had heard of them, but had never seen them, or owned one. She had heard that there was one near her village, and that it was dangerous. She added that she had heard that mandrake roots were used to attract money, but did not believe that they did, because "My voices have never told me anything about them."

As for her power *over* her voices, Joan explicitly told the Inquisitor: "I am not sure that the voice would obey me, unless it were the will of God," and proceeded to demonstrate that he had misinterpreted her relation with her voices. It was not she who forced the voices to come to her. It was they who would speak to her before she "invoked" them. They would, at times, even wake her. She also pointed out, of course, that she would pray for them to come if she felt she needed them and they were not present. She added that they did not always immediately respond to her prayers even though they were always with her when she needed them. She added, "I believe firmly, just as I profess the Catholic faith and believe in the redemption of the soul by divine grace from the suffering of hell, yes, I believe that the Voice comes to me from God and by His will." The voice came when God, and not she, wanted them to.

When Cauchon's questioning led to the matter of amulets, or other objects which could have been *magical,* Joan turned the tables on the Inquisitor. When the court asked Joan if she had ever prayed for her sword, Joan retorted, "Really, now! You think I tried to bewitch my weapons!" When they asked her if she was wont to wear rings, on the other hand, she replied:

> You have taken one of my rings! Give it back! The Burgundians took the other ring. If you have it, show it to me. . . . I believe the names of Jesus and Mary were engraved on it. I don't know who had the names engraved; but as far as I remember it did not have precious stones on it. The ring was given to me at Domrémy. My brother gave me another one; you have it, and I ask you please to offer it to the church. I have never healed anyone with my rings.[14]

Her standard came up time and time again, the standard that portrayed Christ. The Inquisitor asked her if she had ever had it blessed with holy water. Joan replied that she had not. He asked her if she preferred her standard or her sword, and she responded that she vastly preferred her standard to her sword[15]—the magical sword which had been found under the altar of the chapel of St. Catherine at Fierbois. Upon the court's request, she then explained that she had had the standard made on God's command, and carried it personally into battle very simply because she did not want to kill anyone:

"How many times do I have to tell you that I did what I did by the will of God? I carried my own standard when I went to battle, because I did not want to kill anyone. I never killed anyone." The point is that Joan denied all of the Inquisitor's insinuations that she considered her rings, swords, or any other part of her accouterment to be amulets.

Joan's youth and sex came up time and time again at her trial. The Inquisitor attempted to use both the budding sexuality, attributable to a thirteen-year-old girl, and the masculine nature of the quest, to which the voices called Joan, to discredit her experiences. He asked Joan many questions regarding the way in which her *voices* appeared to her. Was St. Michael fully dressed—scales and all—when she saw him, or was he naked when he appeared? What especially interested him was whether Joan touched or had physical contact with her visions, what *part* of the voices she touched, and her reactions to physical contact with the voices. He also specifically asked Joan whether she wanted to be a man and whether she felt that it was proper for her to do a man's job. Questions such as these clearly aimed to ascertain, both whether Joan's apparitions had any sexual significance for her and whether she did have uncommon sexual tendencies.

To the latter questions, Joan simply answered that she had no desire to be a man, but that it was God's pleasure to use her, a simple maid, as an instrument to free France. She added that she had had no desire to do a man's job. She pointed out that when she did do shepherding, or bring the cattle out, for instance, it was not because she did so habitually after she had grown up, but because there was a real need to—when there was fear of an attack. And when she was asked why she dressed like a man she responded, "It was necessary for me to wear men's clothes. I believe that those who directed me to wear them did well." And, "Everything I have done was by God's will. If He were to command me to dress differently, I would do it because it is He who commands it."

As for the manner in which the voices appeared to her, after having told the court that she would not describe what the voices looked like, she added, "We tell our children that 'people are sometimes hanged for telling the truth.' " Joan then had fun showing the Inquisition just how foolish its questions were. The dialogue between Joan and the court regarding the nakedness—and hairlessness—of her voices has rightly become famous:

Court: "What did St. Michael look like when he appeared to you? . . . Was he naked?"

Joan: "Do you think that God does not have the wherewithal to clothe him?"

Court: "Did he have hair?"

Joan: "Why would one cut it off?"

Her point was that it is ridiculous to use human standards to describe angels. But the court insisted: "Do you think that the archangels Michael and Gabriel look like human beings?" To which Joan responded, "I saw them with my eyes and I believe that those whom I saw are they, just as I believe that God exists." Joan did admit that seeing her voices gave her great joy. "Every time I see St. Michael, I feel great joy; it seems to me, when I see him, that I am no longer in a state of sin."

After the preliminary sessions, Joan also admitted that she had physical contact with her voices, saying that she had embraced both St. Catherine and St. Margaret. The court excitedly asked her what part of her *voices* she embraced, to which Joan stated that she embraced them as it was proper for her to do: around their lower parts, by which she intended the legs, of course.[16] Other parts, which were perhaps the ones Cauchon was attempting to have Joan admit to having had contact with, are in the middle of the body.

The Inquisitor discovered all sorts of paradoxes emerge in attempting to characterize Joan's *voices* sexually. If Joan's visions did have a hidden erotic source, and if this is the sense in which one interprets the appearance of a *male* figure in her first mystical experience (the problem here being that angels do not have a gender), it is curious that Joan then turned around to do a "man's" job at the voice's urging. One would expect Joan to have had a more feminine response to a masculine presence, if her relation to that presence was indeed sexual. If, on the other hand, Joan's tendency was to homosexuality, why was the first voice that appeared to her a male voice? And so on. The Inquisitor's reaction to the paradoxes was the educated one. He abandoned the line of questioning.

Hints were even made regarding the possible hysterical origin of her voices. Joan was asked if she had ever met Catherine de la Rochelle, who also claimed to have visions of a *Dame Blanche*, a woman in white, who came to her at night, and what she thought of that case. She responded:

> I asked Catherine if that lady visited her every night and told her that I would sleep with her one night to see her. I did it, I lay awake until midnight and did not see a thing. Then I fell asleep. When day broke, I asked her if the lady had come; she told me that she had, but that I was sleeping and that she had not been able to wake me up. . . . So I slept that day in order to stay awake at night. . . . I saw nothing despite the fact that I often asked her if the lady would come, and Catherine always responded that she would.[17]

Thus, Joan concluded, she thought it best for Catherine to return to her husband, to do her housework, and to feed her children. For, there was no substance to her visions. They were folly. "In order to be absolutely sure, I asked St. Margaret and St. Catherine, who told me that Catherine's whole story was pure folly," Joan told the Inquisitor. [18]

Joan's responses to the Inquisitor's questions reveal not just that she was painfully aware of the direction in which his lines of questioning were leading—of the apparent impropriety of her quest, of the similarity between her experience and purely delusional behavior—but that she was capable of distinguishing delusional visions from true visions.

It could be argued that no delusional visionary would be willing to admit the authenticity of another's visions, and as such, that Joan's claim that Catherine was a fraud does not indicate that she was capable of distinguishing real visions from wish fulfilling ones, but that she felt threatened by Catherine. (After their encounter, Catherine also claimed that Joan was a fraud.) Delusional visionaries, however, do not tend to be willing to give other visionaries any credit at all. There is, for instance, no account of Catherine asking Joan to partake in her visions. But there is testimony that Joan did, and as such that she did take Catherine's claim seriously. Furthermore, people with wish-fulfilling visions do not tend to withhold information regarding those visions. Catherine de la Rochelle was more than willing to describe everything about her visions: what was said, what they looked like, when they came, and things of this sort. Joan was not.

Joan let her judges understand that she herself had had doubts regarding the authenticity and origin of her own visions. It took her three times to believe that the voice she heard was the Archangel Michael's. She had clearly doubted the authenticity of the voice the first two times. She had told her voice that she could not possibly do what it asked since she had never ridden or waged war.[19] She clearly questioned the voice's power, its origin. Joan had had doubts similar to the Inquisitor's regarding her voices.

Joan's recognition of the validity of her visions was rational. Her responses to Cauchon's line of questioning reveal that as easy as it is to raise questions about, and objections to, Joan's claim that she was given a sacred mission by God directly, it is by no means a simple matter to make those objections hold. Not only were Joan's responses to the Inquisitor's questions too rational to warrant the accusation of delusional behavior, her specific responses—as well as her behavior—rule out Cauchon's own, and the many subsequent attempts to do so. If Joan suffered any serious physical problems it is improbable that she could have lead the physically taxing life of a medieval soldier. It is very unlikely indeed that she had Ménière's disease. Ménière's disease causes such serious equilibrium problems, it rules out riding a horse, scaling walls, and other such activities. As for chromosomal abnormalities; there is no evidence to substantiate it.

The evidence of witchcraft is also very tenuous. More than the insignificance of the evidence in the theory's favor, however, is the mass of solid evidence which rules it out. Joan gave every sign of being a very devout Catholic. Cauchon knew this. Not only did she constantly beg the Inquisitor to be given the sacraments—which one might perhaps claim was solicited behavior—she went to mass on every occasion that she had. There is a long list of unsolicited masses she attended. On her way to Chinon, her party stopped in Auxerre in order to go to mass; she went to three masses at Fierbois on that same trip. Joan also had her own personal confessor, the mendicant monk Jean Pasquerel. His testimony relates just how devout a Catholic Joan was; she confessed frequently and she took Communion frequently. She also called her men to confess before a battle. Behavior such as this is not easy to reconcile with sorcery, especially the kind which Cauchon and others have attempted to attribute to Joan.

What these and all other attempts to attribute some cause—other than God—to Joan's deeds have in common is the recognition of the fact that Joan did indeed perform extraordinary deeds and that all extraordinary deeds require extraordinary causes. Scholars and others concede that she was not a *normal* person, and that her deeds required something other than a normal cause. What they do not agree upon is the nature of the *abnormal* cause of her deeds.

Extraordinary deeds do require extraordinary causes. But the extraordinary causes must also be proportionate to the extraordinary deeds. And what most attempts to define the cause of Joan's extraordinary deeds fail to do is come up with a cause which is proportionate to her deeds. The most important—and difficult—matter to account for in Joan is her power. Joan was magnetic. Not only did she have the strength to change the mood of the entire Armagnac party, she also convinced thousands of soldiers to change their mores—to attend mass and live without the female attachments to which medieval armies were assuaged. She convinced her army to seek spiritual purity. It is especially astounding that she managed to convince Charles of Valois to fight.

It is this power that makes psychological and physiological analysis of Joan ineffectual. They cannot explain the most important matter at hand: how Joan got that power. Even if Joan did have Ménière's disease, which is highly unlikely, that disease could not account for her magnetism. The one thing that disease does cause necessarily is terrible physical discomfort. And terrible physical discomfort is not magnetism, or the necessary cause of it; rather it would more likely block magnetism and drain one's power to concentrate. Psychological and physiological analyses of Joan seem to miss the real point. Listing the possible causes of Joan's having heard voices, and things of this sort is not very helpful, when it comes to understanding Joan. What's needed is an explanation of how she got her power.

Joan's power could have been produced by one of two things: Joan herself—some capacity of her own—or something other than herself. But if the source of that power had been Joan herself—as those who question the divine origin of her mission somehow imply—then it is unimaginable that she would have behaved as she did at Rouen. With that amount of power she would have escaped from her jail in Rouen. There is no question about the fact that she wanted to escape.[20] And that desire could only have increased as the trial neared the stake. Joan was terrified of dying, especially at the stake.

Joan attempted to escape from Beaurevoir, Jean de Luxembourg's castle, at least twice. Joan would as such have used her power to escape if it had indeed been in her control. The fact that she did not, indicates that she was not the source of her power. One could object that Joan's power was not of the physical kind, and that physical power is exactly the sort which she would have needed to escape from her Rouen jail. This is not true. There are many ways of escaping from prison, and the best ones require no more than the power of persuasion. And this is exactly the kind of power Joan had. Joan convinced thousands upon thousands of people to follow her.

If Joan had been the source of her own power, then there is no explaining why she did not use that power to convince a mere handful of judges to let her go. What are seventy men in comparison to the thousands that Joan had in her command? This suggests that Joan could not have been the source of her own power, but that that source, as she herself claimed, was God.

Cauchon knew this—he was a trained academic. After six sessions in which Joan's interrogation took place publicly, Cauchon, who had promised a beautiful trial, was baffled. He realized that rather than giving him something of which to accuse her, Joan's interrogations were actually demonstrating that she was a holy quester. He therefore decided to try an abrupt change of strategy: to have Joan be interrogated her prison cell rather than a public courtroom; to increase the number of daily interrogations, and to cut down the number of interrogators. This new form of interrogation began on March 10.

These new interrogations would force Joan to spend her entire days in her cell where she was to not only made to wear ankle chains, but had the added misfortune of being chained to a wooden block. Cauchon's hope was clearly to wear Joan down psychologically. He also put another kind of pressure on her; he withheld the sacraments from her, despite her constant request to receive them. This was probably the thing that made Joan suffer the most.

His tactic did meet with some success. After the interrogations were moved to her cell, Joan's blunt answers—her "yeas," "nays," and "spare me"—and bold ones, were replaced with allegorical ones. On the matter of the sign which she claimed to have shown Charles of Valois at Chinon, for instance, on March 1, she was asked if there were an angel over Charles's head when she first saw him, to which she replied "By the Blessed Mary, if there was I don't know, I didn't see it." On March 10, Joan was once again asked about the sign. She was pointedly asked if it were something material, a crown or something. On that day she answered that the sign was "honorable . . . and good, and the richest thing in the whole world." She added that it "still existed and would last a thousand years."

It is difficult to know what Joan meant by any of her allegories. The one on the king's sign, for instance, became more elaborate as time went on. At a certain point, she even claimed that the king's sign smelled good. What seems certain is that the allegories were her new response to the additional pressure Cauchon had put on her. One can afford to be brash when one is in public, and can get the members of an oversized court to argue among themselves and laugh at each other, which is exactly what Joan quickly became a master at. Her answers in the first sessions are caustic and funny. They ridiculed the questions she was asked, and above all, had the specific purpose of dividing the court. Her response to the question, "Are you in a state of grace" has justly become a classic example of her tactic. To that question Joan responded: "If I am may God keep me in it. If I am not, may he put me in it." One cannot, however, be so brash when one is interrogated in private by four judges. Four people can easily close ranks and gang up against another person. Joan therefore changed tactics: She gave the Inquisitors enigmatic answers, and plenty of them.

Not even the change in tactic gave Cauchon much to pin on Joan. After a month of interrogations, he finally had Jean d'Estivet draw up a list of articles of indictment. Estivet came up with seventy. Most of them were based upon twisted accounts of Joan's own testimony. Joan's claim that she was taught the catholic faith by her mother, became the charge that she had been taught "sorcery, divination" and other pagan things. For Domrémy was a "pagan" town. Her claim that she had never owned, or even seen a mandrake root, became the charge that she wore a mandrake root under her shirt.

There were several serious charges. One had to do with her male dress, which the court claimed to be blasphemous. One had to do with the fact that she had not consulted any member of the Church hierarchy on the matter of her voices. The most serious of them all was that she refused to submit to the Church Militant on the matter of her voices and behavior. Namely, that she refused to let the Church Militant judge whether her voices came from God, but obstinately claimed that they did. And, she had refused to allow the Church Militant to judge whether what the voices had called her to do was right, but took that task upon herself. The Church Militant in question was, of course, Cauchon's inquisitorial court. For Joan had asked to be brought to the pope.

The seventy articles were read to Joan on March 27 and 28, who had a chance to respond to them. In the following week the seventy articles were condensed to twelve. This was done by Nicholas Midi of the University of Paris. The articles were reviewed by a party of assessors. Several were wary of giving their assent to the proceedings, and more or less stated that Joan's statements could be qualified as evil only if her voices had not come from God, and that Cauchon had not established that they had not. Others called for the case to be sent to Rome, to the pope. On April 12, however, the University of Paris gave Cauchon its approval for the articles. And that was enough for him.

In the meanwhile, Joan had fallen deathly ill. She claimed to have been poisoned by Cauchon. The English were furious. They were afraid that she might escape public execution after they had paid so much for the proceedings. When the doctors came, the earl of Warwick warned them not to bleed her: "Take care, She is cunning and might well kill herself."[21] Joan, on the other hand, asked for the sacraments. She was afraid that she would die. The court responded that they would give her the sacraments only if she submitted to the Church Militant on the matter of her voices. Joan responded that she loved God and wished that the Church would pray for her. She was not given the sacraments.

Joan was, however, warned to submit to the Church Militant again, on May 2. On that occasion Joan made a subtle distinction, and claimed that she believed fully in the Church Militant, but on the matter of her voices she relied on God, who had called her to do what she had done. She added that she would respond to the pope regarding her voices. This was not the first time she had asked to be brought to the pope. While the articles of indictment were being read to her:

> Joan was being pressed to submit to the church, she replied that she would willingly submit to the Holy Father, and asked to be taken to him, but she did not wish to submit to those who were there, because they were her principal enemies. I intervened to advise her to submit to the Council General at Basel . . . [because] there were as many of her party as of the party of the English. Hearing this Joan began to say . . . "I should like to go and submit to the Council of Basel." Immediately, reproaching me with great spite and indignation, the Bishop of Beauvais cried: "Be silent, for the devil's sake." Then the notary, Guillaume Manchon, asked if he should register Joan's submission to the Council. The bishop told him no . . . and that he must not write it down. At which Joan said to the bishop: "Ha! You write well enough what goes against me, and do not write what is for me."[22]

On May 9, Joan was threatened with torture. But still she did not submit to the court's judgement on the matter of her voices. Cauchon was at a loss. He thus deferred to the University of Paris once again. On May 14 he sent his colleagues a copy of the twelve articles, without any of the supporting documents. They replied on May 19: Joan was a dangerous liar who consorted with devils.

On May 24, Cauchon came up with his most brilliant plan. He took Joan to the cemetery of St. Ouen, where he had had several platforms and a large scaffold built. In front of a large crowd—which included the very young Henry VI—he told Joan that she would burn if she did not submit to the Church Militant. Joan once again asked to be brought to the pope. "I appeal to God and to our Holy Father the pope." She was ignored and told that the pope was too far away to be called upon.

Instead, they presented her with a cedula on which someone had penned some sort of an abjuration. Joan did not know what was on the slip of paper; she was illiterate. She claimed not to know how to write, and then laughed and signed the paper with a cross. It's unknown what was written on the cedula. Jean Massieu claimed that it was seven lines long and that it merely said that Joan promised never to dress in men's clothing, crop her hair, or carry arms again. The document that sits in archives is a long and very damning piece, which among other things, claims that Joan was a fraud and that she never heard voices.

The general reaction to her laughter was that she did not take the abjuration seriously. Cauchon was specifically rebuked on the point. That she did not take it seriously would seem to be corroborated by the fact that she signed the cedula with a cross. Joan herself told the court that she did not mean for documents signed with a cross to be taken seriously. But her abjuration was taken seriously. She was given women's clothes, changed, was thrown back in prison, and her head was shaven.

Three days later, Joan had changed back into men's clothes. How was she able to do so? Leggings are impossible to put on when one is chained by both ankles. There was clearly someone who wanted Joan to change back into men's clothing. Given what is known of the cedula she signed—that is, that she promised not to change back into men's clothing—it must be supposed that that someone wanted her to relapse.

That there was an accomplice was corroborated by Joan herself, who claimed that she woke up on the morning of May 28 to find that her dress had disappeared, and that the only clothes she could put on were men's clothes.[23] When Cauchon entered her cell and asked her why she had relapsed, Joan responded that, "I did it of my own will. I took it again because it was more lawful and convenient than to have women's clothes because I am with men. I began to wear them again, because what was promised me was not observed, to wit that I should go to mass and receive the body of Christ and be freed from these irons."

When Cauchon asked her if she had heard her voices since Thursday, May 24, Joan responded that she had and that, "God has expressed through St. Catherine and St. Margaret His great sorrow at the strong treason to which I consented in abjuring and making a revocation to save my life, and said that I was damning myself to save my life." With those words Joan practically signed her death warrant. The recorder noted as much in the margin of his notes: *responsio mortifera*.

Two days later, Joan was condemned to death and burnt at the stake. That morning, a monk, Martin Ladvenu heard her confession, and Joan asked for the Eucharist. Ladvenu was not sure whether he should give it to her—she was excommunicated. He consulted Cauchon, who told the Dominican to "give her the sacrament of the Eucharist and anything she asks."

13

Nations Lost and Found

France shall do the greatest feat of arms
that was ever done for Christianity.

—*Joan of Arc*

Over five and one half centuries have passed since Joan's death,
and yet we are still writing books about her, asking ourselves
who she really was, what she really did, and why what she did
was so important. It is the facts which give us the best answer to
the first two questions.

Before Joan appeared, France was a depressed place, which
was on the verge of falling under foreign domination. And that
not so much because the Treaty of Troyes had officially made
Henry of England the heir to the French throne—treaties are
more often than not broken—but because of the general feeling
of the people in France. The French were convinced that they
were going to fall under English rule.

The despondent attitude of the French had many causes. One
of them was, most certainly, the apparent invincibility of the
English: Agincourt and Crépy were realities. The English had literally trounced the French, and the French—those, that is, who
had not allied with the English—did not believe that they were
capable of retaliating. This is one of the first things Joan learned
when she began to participate in the war. Every one of the battles in which she participated was prefaced by a council of war

which invariably came to the conclusion that Armagnac soldiers were too few to put up a serious fight against the English. The constancy of Armagnac captains on this matter is almost boring.

The captains were not the only ones who thought that they were incapable of winning. Armagnac troops seemed to retreat at the speed of light in all of their battles; all it took was a small peep on the part of the English to make them run. Joan knew this too. One of her most important roles on the battlefield was to call retreating soldiers back to the fight. It was she who charged ahead when the Armagnacs were about to let their attempt to seize the Augustins founder—she called the fleeing French to follow her in God's name. It was under her banner that the Tourelles were captured. As it was, once, again, she who reversed the Armagnac retreat at Jargeau.

French despondence was, however, also caused by the lack of real leaders in the Armagnac ranks. Charles of Valois, whom one would have expected to want to lead the fight against the English, had retreated to Bourges long before he met Joan, and showed no signs of wanting to lay any serious claim to the throne of France. He seemed content with his mock court and the disparaging title of "king of Bourges." He was a rather pusillanimous little man, as his attempted flight to the Loire in the aftermath of his coronation demonstrates. Nor was there anyone to take Charles's place, to do his fighting for him. The duke of Orléans was being held hostage in England, and the other potential leaders of the Armagnac resistance—Dunois, d'Alençon, and whoever else there was—were either busy paying off their ransoms, or too frightened to make convincing leaders.

The dearth of leaders in the Armagnac ranks points to the most serious thing lacking in France before Joan came to the scene: a sense of nationhood. At the turn of the fifteenth century, there was no real kingdom of France—at least as we conceive of a kingdom. France, at that time, was a series of counties, duchies, and baronies, and the people of France were loyal to their counts, dukes, and barons. They fought in the armies of their counts, dukes, and barons and they identified with their counts, dukes, and barons. They were Burgundians, Barrois, Provençals, Normans, or what not. They did not, however, consider themselves or their lands French. Joan herself showed signs of this. Throughout her trial, Joan referred to her journey from Domrémy as her "coming to France." What her statements imply, of course, is that Domrémy is not France.

The fact that there was no sense of nationhood in France before Joan appeared had serious consequences. One of them was that it let the Hundred Years' War become a civil war. It's because the duke of Burgundy (and his people) did not feel that he owed allegiance to the king—or to a larger nation—that he allied with the English. It is also why he seemed to feel no guilt at killing the Armagnacs. The lack of a real sense of nationhood also explains why the people of France did not constantly rebel at the prospect of falling under English rule. Their allegiance lay with their counts, dukes, barons, and so forth, and the Treaty of Troyes did not call for a change in local nobility.

All of this changed after Joan appeared. With Joan's arrival, the Armagnacs lost their fear. They emerged from their depression. Thousands upon thousands of men flocked to her side to help her throw off the yoke of foreign domination. Once Joan appeared, the Armagnacs did not flee once they saw the English. They were even seriously tempted to attack their foes when they were at their most fearsome—in battle formation. After Joan, the people of France began to rebel at the prospect of falling under English rule. Town after town began to throw out the English garrisons stationed within their walls, and pay homage to Charles of Valois. After Joan, the people of France began to consider themselves French and not primarily Armagnacs or Burgundians; they swore fealty to their king. With Joan's arrival, French resistance had a leader—the people a cohesive force. Duby, the medieval historian, makes the point succinctly:

Her brief appearance on the political scene had extraordinary repercussions. Although she had died, with her intervention the tide had suddenly and miraculously turned. Despair was banished, and even her death could not check the movement that she had initiated. It was to lead to the liberation of France from English occupation twenty years later.[1]

Joan, in other words, taught her people to rise above their petty concerns and provincialism and see that there was a larger unity that needed to be made out of each of the provinces of France. She showed the people of France that making this larger unity was their own responsibility, and that they could make it if they fought for it. She proclaimed that the larger unity was a sacred thing—that it was a response to a divine calling. She pointed out that the larger unity of France had a mission. And the response that Joan received from the people of France demonstrates just how right she was. Joan was not just the moving cause of France. She is in some sense the embodiment of France itself. Joan is the expression of the spirit that made its people build those glorious cathedrals that soar over their countryside still today.

The cathedrals have a kind of proud beauty; theirs is the beauty of might. They are not timid buildings. There is nothing Franciscan about them. They are monuments to the power, wonder, and glory of their God. Joan's beauty is of the same kind. She met all of the obstacles she was presented with a confidence, which almost seems to border on arrogance. It isn't hard to imagine her marching into Baudricourt's castle demanding an escort and never doubting that she would get one. Nor did she waste time on careful phrasing when she spoke to the high and mighty. She was as blunt as a person can be, even when her life was in danger.

Cathedrals are not quiet buildings; they are not serene. Theirs is not the classical beauty of the Greek temple. They are the embodiment of the struggle for clarity, of the joy of the quest, of the fierce passion of running, singing, and jumping, of climbing the high mountain. Historians to the contrary, Joan did not only express her faith on her knees or in the ecstatic poses typified by nineteenth century portraits of the saints. Joan was a doer. She was a great captain and an energetic warrior. Dunois and d'Alençon both testified to that effect.[3] They even added that her specialty, as far as military tactics are concerned, was artillery. She was especially masterful at placing cannons.[3]

Cathedrals are also symphonies of contrasts. The apparent delicacy of their interiors, of their traceries, their stained glass windows, is balanced by the extraordinary jungle of buttresses and counterbuttresses on their exteriors. Their incredible—almost effortless—interior suspension is balanced by the massive real struggle one sees in their exteriors. And so too was Joan a symphony of contrasts. For that very same girl who rode with ease and jousted with elegance was the leader of an army. That very same girl who couched the lance, who fretted when she was held back, who wanted to fight, cried when she saw the ugly aftermath of a battle.

And just as Joan was like the cathedrals, so too did she embody that other great expression of the spirit of France: chivalry. This has been pointed out before.[4] Like the knights of old, Joan followed an honor code to which she was fiercely attached. She sent three letters to the English garrisoned at Orléans, for instance, to warn them of her intentions. This was dictated by the code. Like the knights of old, she even had a special sword.[5]

In some obscure sense, Joan is France. That is why the French have rallied under her banner for the five hundred and fifty-odd years that separate us from her death, despite the radical changes that the nation has undergone since then.[6] Both the Monarchists and the Liberals of the nineteenth century laid claim to her, and called people to join their causes in her name. Soldiers were called to defend France in her name in World War I. In her honor, De Gaulle made the emblem of Free France the cross of

Lorraine in World War II. Her name is still being used as a battle cry by French politicians today.

Joan's quest, by her own admission, was divinely inspired. Joan claimed to have done nothing as far as the liberation of France was concerned, which was not commanded by God. This implies that God wanted France to belong to the French—that he wanted France to be a nation. This is a very strong claim, which would surely make even the most ardent of French atheists grin with delight still today. French nationalism has become legendary. It certainly had many of Joan's rehabilitation judges nodding vigorously with approval. Elie de Bourdeilles, the Bishop of Perigueux and one of these judges, made the point succinctly:

> This girl . . . was sent for the liberation and consolation of the king and kingdom. . .and in the service of God she liberated the kingdom from the hands of the English, with God compassionately cooperating, as one can piously believe.[7]

But Joan's claim that God wanted France to be a nation implies that nationhood itself can be sacred. It suggests that there is a divine order behind what the modern mind tends to consider coincidental unities of peoples. It implies that the evolution of society has a goal to which it tends; that there is a divine plan behind human history.

Both history and philosophy make these implications troublesome. And not just because history has shown that a nation can be formed by a unity of people who do not share the same religious creed, and thus allow us to infer that Church and State, religion and country, are different things, but more basically, because nationhood seems to lack one of the prerequisites of a sacred unity. A nation is not just a unity of people. It is a unity of people who live within specific geographic boundaries and who share a specific common culture. It is a unity from which those people who do not live within the nation's geographic boundaries and who do not share the nation's culture are necessarily excluded. And a unity of this kind seems to be a far cry from the unity of people called for by religion, from a sacred unity. A sacred unity is one from which no one is necessarily excluded. It is one which transcends borders and cultures.

What makes Joan's claim even more difficult to accept are the vicissitudes of history. If a nation is indeed a sacred thing, a unity called for and protected by God, can we then infer that the success of one nation with respect to another is sanctioned by God? Can we infer that God has favorites?

These questions are not original. The Inquisitor at Rouen came up with them long before we did. He was especially interested in the matter of God's playing favorites. He pointedly asked Joan if her voices could speak English,[8] and if God—and his messengers—hated the English,[9] showing that he had more than just intuited the problem.

But Joan, too, understood the problem, as her saucy responses to Cauchon's questions show. She told the Inquisitor that her voices naturally spoke in French, since they sided with the French.[10] And as for their hating the English, they naturally loved what God loved. But she did not know whether God hated the English or not. She was only sure that he would drive them out of France, "excepting, of course, those who would die there."[11]

Cauchon was, however, also interested in the more basic matter of nationhood. He had, after all, helped his colleagues at the University of Paris formulate the double monarchy theory, which justified the Treaty of Troyes: the English takeover of France. And his theory, at least as far as he was concerned, demonstrated that it was God's own will that the kingdoms of France and England be united. For, he claimed, since the division of the two kingdoms had led to war, sedition, and the diminution of faith; their union would bring about the immediate cessation of hostilities and usher in a new age of hope.[12]

Thus when Cauchon came face to face with the person who not only negated his theory, but also claimed that she was doing so in God's name, he did his utmost to prove that she was wrong. But was she?

Cauchon's solution was to attempt to refute the major premise of Joan's claim—to prove that Joan's mission was not divinely inspired. But his attempt to do so was not very successful. For the Inquisitor not only substituted the abjuration cedula, which Joan signed in the cemetery of St. Ouen, replacing it with the one we now have, he also tried to have some last statements—which he claimed Joan to have made on the morning of her death—added to the official transcript of her trial a week after her death. The statements naturally contain a complete abjuration on Joan's part. Unfortunately for the Archbishop, however, the notaries refused to authenticate the statements—they called his bluff.

Cauchon would never have resorted to such tactics if he had been successful in his attempt to prove that Joan was not what she purported to be. Such tactics were beneath his dignity. Above all, they left him open to future attack. One surmises, as such, that some part of him must have felt defeated by Joan.

But if Joan was right, are we to infer that God does want nations, that nations are in some sense a part of his plan? If this is so, then what are we to make of Constantinople? The Hundred Years' War ended in the very same year that Constantinople fell. In 1453, one nation was saved and one perished. But how can this be if nations are a sacred thing? Why did God not aid that glorious old last lingering echo of the ancient world, if nations are a part of his plan? Why didn't God send Byzantium a Joan?

In the early 1440s, John VIII, emperor of Constantinople, knew that his people were in danger; his enemies were on his borders. He set out to western Europe with an entire retinue of theologians to try to patch things up with Rome. For he felt that the West would help him save his people, his culture, if the great schism of Christianity were brought to an end. He and his retinue settled in Florence and had the most important forgotten council of the Church.

The stunning end of the council was the Emperor's decree: that the eastern Church give its oath of obedience to Rome. He had, he felt, done his part. The West would have to fight to protect its own kindred in faith. And what ensued is one of the most tragic episodes in our history. The West did virtually nothing.

Would this have happened if the Hundred Years' War had not been going on? If two of the key kingdoms of the Catholic West had not been fighting each other? Probably not. Joan herself claimed that she wanted to go on a crusade. She had even invited the English to participate in it two years before she died, in May of 1429:

> You, duke of Bedford, the Maid begs and requires of you that you discontinue the destruction. If you grant her right, you may still come into her company where the French shall do the greatest feat of arms that was ever done for Christianity. And make answer if you wish to make peace in the city of Orléans; and if you do not do so, may you be reminded of it by your great injuries.

Joan told Charles at Chinon that she needed to work fast: she only had a year, hardly more. She also warned her dauphin that if he did not allow her to follow her own voices, he would only be able to regain his nation after a long and bitter struggle. She was, of course, right. Joan was burnt at the stake in 1431. The Hundred Years' War ended in 1453. It took Charles twenty more years to free his land.

Joan's death, as such, teaches us as much as her life does. For Joan was betrayed. There can be no doubt about this. Charles of Valois may not personally have delivered her to the Anglo-Burgundians, but he was certainly glad that she was gone. And he was certainly responsible for her death. He made no move to ransom her in all of the months that she was held in the castle of Beaurevoir. She was certainly not the first person whom Charles betrayed. But Charles's betrayal of Joan was a crucial one: It shows the effects of a people's not heeding its calling.

ACKNOWLEDGEMENTS

Writing a book on Joan of Arc is a real challenge today. There have been so many good books about Joan written in the last five hundred years, that simply sifting through the material is a frightening thing. I therefore want to thank the many people who gave me the courage to do so. To Antonia, my most heartfelt thanks, for her challenging readings, stimulating comments, and historical savvy. To Carlo, my gratitude for the technological support, and psychoanalytic expertise. To Bronwyn, thank you for the music and the Saturday discussions. To Mary, Tona, and Joelle, thanks for the comic book, and the help. To Luisa, my deep appreciation for organizing the Joan lecture at the University of Padova. To Timmie and Paul, my thanks for the discussions. To Maria, thank you for listening to my endless office talk on Joan. To Father Joe, thank you for being you. To my mother and father my gratitude for their input. To my sisters and brothers, nieces and nephews, my special thanks. I must also thank Eireanne, who took the day to help me with the chronology.

CHRONOLOGY

Jan. 6, 1412	Joan's conventional birthday
1425	Joan begins to hear voices
May 1428	Joan's first visit to Vaucouleurs
July 1428	Anglo-Burgundian raid on Domrémy Joan in Neufchâteau
Oct. 12, 1428	Anglo-Burgundian siege on Orléans begins
Jan. 1429	Joan's second visit to Vaucouleurs
Feb. 12, 1429	Joan leaves for Chinon
Feb. 1429	Joan meets Charles of Valois, dauphin of France
March 23, 1429	Poitiers commission declares Joan to be a pious Catholic with a divine mission
April 27, 1429	Joan departs for Orléans to raise the siege
April 29, 1429	Joan arrives at Orléans

1377 End of "Avignon Captivity" of the popes
1384 Flanders become part of the duchy of Burgundy
Early 1400s
   Flowering of Renaissance of Art in Florence: Brunelleschi (1377–1446), Ghiberti (1378–1455), Paolo Uccello (1396–1477) . . . Philosophy: Rebirth of Platonism: Marsilio Ficino (1433–99) Nicholas of Cusa (1401–64)
   Invention of Printing Press: Guttenberg (1400–68)
1405 Venice (Republica Serenissima) conquers northwestern Italy
1407 Bethlehem Hospital, London (Bedlam) becomes institution for the insane
1411 Founding of St. Andrews University, Edinburgh

1414 End of Western Schism of the Church: Council of Constance
   Martin V declared pope
1416 The Medici of Florence become bankers to the papacy
1419 War of the Hussites
1420 Treaty of Troyes: Henry V heir to the French throne
   Burgundians lose battle of Mont S. Michel
   University of Louvain founded
1426 Holland becomes the center of European music

1429 Henry VI crowned at Westminster
   Philip of Burgundy creates the Order of the Golden Fleece

May 4, 1429	Battle for St. Loup
May 6, 1429	Battle for the Augustins
May 7, 1429	Battle for the Tourelles
May 8, 1429	Orléans completely freed
June 9, 1429	Beginning of the Loire expedition
June 12, 1429	Jargeau captured
June 15, 1429	Meung capitulates
June 17, 1429	Capitulation of Beaugency
June 18, 1429	Battle of Patay
June 25, 1429	Joan marches for Gien
June 29, 1429	The coronation march begins
July 1, 1429	Coronation party reaches Auxerre
July 5, 1429	Coronation party reaches Troyes
July 10, 1429	Capitulation of Troyes
July 14, 1429	Coronation party reaches Châlons
July 17, 1429	Coronation of Charles VII of Valois
Aug. 2, 1429	Charles announces truce with duke of Burgundy
Aug. 25, 1429	Joan in St. Denis: prepares for the attack on Paris
Sept. 8, 1429	Attack on Paris
Sept. 10, 1429	Retreat from Paris
Sept. 21, 1429	Charles VII disbands the royal army
Oct. 1429	Joan is in Bourges
Oct. 1429	Preparations for attacks on St. Pierre, La Charité
Dec. 1429	Retreat from La Charité
	Joan is ennobled
Jan. 1430	Joan is in Orléans
March 1430	Joan with a small band of men attack Melun
	Joan's voices warn of her imminent capture
May 23, 1430	Joan is captured in Compiègne
June-Nov. 1430	Joan is held prisoner by Jean de Luxembourg
Dec. 1430	Joan is sold to the English
Jan. 1431	Joan's trial begins
Feb. 21, 1431	Joan's interrogation begins
March 27, 1431	Official indictment of Joan on charges of heresy
May 24, 1431	Joan's "abjuration" at the cemetery of St.-Ouen
May 30, 1431	Joan's execution

1429 Leonardo Bruni finishes his *History of Florence*

1430 Pérez de Guzmán (1376–1460), Span. author, flourished
      Modern English develops from Middle English
      Birth of François Villon (French poet)
      Birth of Andrea Mantegna (Italian painter)

1431 Henry VI of England crowned king of France in Paris
      First German peasant revolt at Worms

1432 Discovery of the Azores

NOTES

CHAPTER 1: THE INQUISITOR AND THE MAID

1. Deposition of Guillaume Manchon, Quicherat III, p. 149.
2. Quicherat II, p. 328.
3. Edward Lucie-Smith, *Joan of Arc*.
4. See, e.g., Anatole France, *La Vie de Jeanne d'Arc*, Paris: 1909.
5. This was, for instance, the opinion Voltaire presented in his mock epic *La Pucelle*.
6. See Anne Llewellyn Barstow, *Joan of Arc: Heretic, Mystic, Shaman*. Barstow contends that Joan was a shaman, who partook in magical practices of the day and hid this fact from her Rouen judges. See p. 49.
7. See Barstow, p. 113. The classic work on this theme is Marina Warner, *Joan of Arc*.
8. On this point see, Naria Margolis, "The 'Joan Phenomenon' and the French Right," in *Fresh Verdicts on Joan of Arc*, pp. 265–288.
9. For an extensive bibliography on Joan of Arc see Nadia Margolis, *Joan of Arc in History, Literature, and Film*.

CHAPTER 2: DOMRÉMY

1. Perceval de Boulainvilliers gave the date in a letter to Filippo Maria Visconti, duke of Milan. Cf. Jean Chartier, *Chronique*, in Jules Quicherat, *Procès de condemnation et de réhabilitation de Jeanne d'Arc, dite la Pucelle*, Paris, 1841–1849, IV, pp. 40–59. See also Frances, Gies, *Joan of Arc: the Legend and the Reality*, p. 10.
2. Domremy actually shifted hands quite often. In Joan's time it was generally held to belong to the royal house of France. Some hundred years later, it became a part of the duchy of Lorraine. It reverted to France some hundred years after that.
3. See Lucie-Smith, pp. 39–40.
4. February 24, 1431, III public session.
5. There is some doubt about this. Some scholars claim that he was

from Arc-en-Barrois, which might explain his last name.

6. See Victoria Sackville-West, *Saint Joan of Arc*, pp. 28–30 on this point.

7. Cf., e.g., deposition of Jean Morel, Quicherat II, p. 388; Deposition of Beatrice Estellin, Quicherat II, p. 395.

8. Deposition of Catherine le Royer, Quicherat II, p. 444.

9. February 24, III public session.

10. Deposition of Jean Waternin, Quicherat II, p. 420.

11. Deposition of Simonin Musnier, Quicherat, II, p. 424.

12. Cf., e.g., deposition of Colin Colin, Quicherat, II, p. 439.

13. Cf. Jean Chartier, *Chronique*, in Quicherat, IV, pp. 40–59.

14. Deposition of Perrin Drappier, Quicherat, II, p. 431.

15. February 22, II public session.

16. February 24, 1431, III public session.

17. Cf., e.g., February 21, 1431, I public session; see also March 12, 1431, prison session.

18. Deposition of Jean Pasquerel, Quicherat III, p. 109.

19. Cf., e.g. February 22, II public session.

20. February 27, 1431, IV public session.

CHAPTER 3: FROM DOMRÉMY TO VAUCOULEURS

1. See deposition of Gérardin Épinal, Quicherat II, p. 423. See also the deposition of Michel Lebuin, Quicherat II, p. 440.

2. March 12, 1431 prison session.

3. March 15, 1431 prison session.

4. Ibid.

5. Deposition of Hauviette, Quicherat II, p. 419.

6. February 24, 1431 public session.

7. March 12, 1431 prison session.

8. Deposition of Colin Colin, Quicherat II, p. 434. It is a matter of debate whether Joan used this excuse for her first visit or her second visit. See Sackville-West, pp. 80–82.

9. There is some contention on this point. The great majority of Joan scholars claim that her first visit to Baudricourt took place in May, 1428. See, e.g., Regine Pernoud, *Joan of Arc: by Herself and her Witnesses*, p. 34; Gies, pp. 31–32. W.S. Scott, on the other hand, argues that it cannot have taken place in May 1428. See *Jeanne d'Arc: Her Life, Death and the Myth*, p. 27.

10. Deposition of Durand Laxart, Quicherat II, p. 444.

11. Quicherat IV, p. 478; Marina Warner, *Image*, pp. 24–26.

12. Cf. Deposition of Jean Barbin, Quicherat, II, pp. 443–444. See also Franco Cardini, *Giovanna d'Arco*, p. 49. The strange thing about this is that the prophecy is not to be found in the twelve volumes of Marie d'Avignon's prophecies.

13. This from Bernard de Poulengy, an eyewitness of that interview. See Quicherat II, p. 456.
14. Deposition of Hauviette, Quicherat II, p. 419.
15. February 22, II public session.
16. Deposition of Marguerite la Tourolde, Quicherat III, p. 87.
17. Deposition of Durand Laxart, Quicherat II, pp. 444–445.
18. Deposition of Jean de Metz, Quicherat II, pp. 436–437.
19. Deposition of Catherine le Royer, Quicherat II, p. 446.
20. Deposition of Durand Laxart, Quicherat II, pp. 444–445.

CHAPTER 4: CHINON

1. Deposition of Henri le Royer, Quicherat II, p. 449.
2. This is a matter of some contention. Some scholars, most notably Sackville-West (p. 112) and W.S. Scott (p. 35) claim that she left on February 24. Others, like Gies claim she left on February 13. See Gies, p. 13. Others yet claim that she left on the 12th. Regine Pernoud is of the latter opinion. Her claim sounds most convincing. See *Joan*, p. 41.
3. See Sackville-West, pp. 107–108.
4. Quicherat I, p. 54. February 22, 1431, II public session.
5. Lucie-Smith, p. 53.
6. February 27, 1431, II public session.
7 See the deposition of Simon Charles, Quicherat III, p. 115.
8. February 27, 1431, IV public session.
9. Quicherat II, pp. 16–17.
10. Jean Chartier, *Chronique*, in Quicherat IV, pp. 52–53.
11. Deposition of Jean Pasquerel, Quicherat III, p. 103.
12. Letter attributed to Alain Chartier, the dauphin's secretary, Quicherat V, p. 133.
13. Sackville-West claims that the prayer had three parts: that Charles would recover his kingdom, that he alone would suffer the consequences of the war, and that the people of France would be forgiven their sins. See pp. 123–124.
14. See Gies, p. 51. Gies proposes a general rereading of Charles's character. History has labeled him as a weak and rather dissolute character, who was often at the mercy of his council. Gies proposes that he was not.
15. February 27, 1431, IV public session.
16. Deposition of Jean Pasquerel, Quicherat III, p. 103.
17. Deposition of Séguin Séguin, Quicherat III, p. 205.
18. Ibid.
19. Deposition of Séguin Séguin, Quicherat III, pp. 204–205.
20. See Antonio Morosini, *Chronique d'Antonio Morosini. Extraits relatifs à l'histoire de France*, Paris, 1898–1902, III, pp. 100–110.
21. Barrett, 165–66. At her Rouen trial, Joan claimed that the letter

as we have it was not quite correct. She had not dictated "surrender to the Maid," but "surrender to God." She had not said "body for body," or described herself as *chef de guerre*.

22. Deposition of Jean Pasquerel, Quicherat III, p. 101–102.
23. February 27, 1431, IV public session.
24. Deposition of Jean d'Alençon, Quicherat III, p. 92.

CHAPTER 5: ORLÉANS

1. A detailed account of the supplies received by the city can be found in the *Journal du Siège d'Orléans*, in Quicherat IV.
2. *Journal du Siège* in Quicherat IV, p. 131. The city even sent a delegation to parley with the Duke. This took place after the disastrous Battle of the Herrings.
3. *Journal du Siège* in Quicherat IV, p. 146.
4. *Journal du Siège* in Quicherat IV, pp. 152–153.
5. Quicherat II, p. 132.
6. Deposition of Dunois, Quicherat III, p. 3.
7. Deposition of Dunois, Quicherat III, p. 4.
8. There were, it seems, 2,000 men in Orléans's garrison and 2,000 in the town's militia. Gies, p. 68.
9. *Journal du Siège* in Quicherat IV, p. 156.
10. *Journal du Siège* in *Journal du Siège* in Quicherat IV, pp. 155–156. See also the Deposition of Dunois, Quicherat III, p. 5.
11. Deposition of Jean d'Aulon, Quicherat III, p. 211.
12. Deposition of Jean Pasquerel, Quicherat III, p. 107.
13. Ibid.
14. Jean Chartier, *Chronique*, in Quicherat IV, p. 57.
15. Deposition of Jean d'Aulon, Quicherat III, p. 214.
16. Deposition of Jean Pasquerel, Quicherat III, p. 109.
17. Deposition of Jean d'Aulon, Quicherat, III, p. 210. There is a bit of a discrepancy here. Both d'Aulon and Simon Charles claim that this event took place on Friday, rather than on Saturday. This is also how Régine Pernoud reads the events in her latest, and last, book on Joan. Cf. Régine Pernoud, *Joan of Arc: Her Story*, p. 45. However, Gies's reading, which places it on Saturday makes more sense.
18. Deposition of Simon Charles, Quicherat III, pp. 116–117.
19. Deposition of Jean Pasquerel, Quicherat III, pp. 109–110.
20. Deposition of Nouillonpont, Quicerat II, p. 438; deposition of Poulegny, Quicherat II, p. 457.
21. *Journal de Siège*, Quicherat IV, p. 160.
22. Deposition of Dunois, Quicherat III, p. 8.
23. Deposition of Dunois, Quicherat III, p. 8; Deposition of Jean d'Aulon, Quicherat III, pp. 216–17; Deposition of Louis de Coutes,

Quicherat III, pp. 70–71.
24. Journal de Siège, Quicherat IV, p. 164.

CHAPTER 6: FROM JARGEAU TO MEUNG

1. Quicherat III, pp. 26–27
2. Quicherat IV, p. 32.
3. *Journal de Siège* in Quicherat IV, p. 152–153.
4. Deposition of Dunois, Quicherat III, p. 13.
5. Deposition of Dunois, Quicherat III, pp. 11–12.
6. The ransom amount was an exorbitant 80,000 gold saluts and was finally paid in full in May, 1429.
7. Quicherat IV, p. 13.
8. Deposition of d'Alençon, Quicherat III, p. 95.
9. Deposition of d'Alençon, Quicherat III, p. 96.
10. Deposition of d'Alençon, Quicherat III, p. 97.
11. Sackville-West, p. 206.
12. Journal de Siège, Quicherat IV, p. 174.
13. Deposition of d'Alençon, Quicherat III, p. 97.
14. Wavrin, *Chroniques*, p. 287–291.
15. Quicherat IV, p. 371.
16. Wavrin, *Chronique*, Quicherat IV, pp. 421–424.

CHAPTER 7: REIMS

1. Deposition of Dunois, Quicherat III, p. 13.
2. *Livre noir de la Rochelle*, Jules Quicherat (ed.), in *Revue historique*, IV, pp. 341–342.
3. Chartrier, *Chronique*, Quicherat IV, p. 71.
4. *Chronique de la Pucelle*, Quicherat IV, p. 248.
5. *Journal du Siège*, Quicherat, IV p. 181.
6. Deposition of Dunois, Quicherat III, p. 13.
7. *Chronique de la Pucelle*, Quicherat IV, p. 252
8. Jean Rogier, Quicherat IV, p. 297.
9. March 3, 1431, VI public session.
10. Jean Rogier, Quicherat IV, p. 298.
11. *Journal du Siège*, Quicherat IV, pp. 184–185.
12. March 1, 1431, V public session.
13. Quicherat V, p. 189.
14. March 3, 1431, VI public session.

CHAPTER 8: PARIS

1. The two towns were tax exempt until 1776.
2. Deposition of Simon Charles, Quicherat III, p. 116.
3. Christine de Pisan, *Ditié de Jehanne d'Arc*, (ed. A.J. Kennedy and K. Varty) Oxford, 1977, pp. 43–44.
4. Christine de Pisan, *Ditié de Jehanne d'Arc*, pp. 30.
5. Parleys began, it seems, on June 30, 1429.
6. Quicherat V, pp. 137–138.
7. Georges Chastellain, *Oevres*, K. De Lettenhove, Brussels, 1863–1865, II, p. 178.
8. Cagny, *Chronique*, Quicherat IV, p. 24.
9. Anonymous chronicler, Quicherat IV, p. 342.
10. Cagny, *Chronique*, Quicherat IV, p. 28.
11. February 27, 1431, IV public session.

CHAPTER 9: THE ROAD TO COMPIÈGNE

1. Cagny, *Chronique*, Quicherat IV, pp. 29–30.
2. Deposition of Margauerite La Touroulde, Quicherat III, p. 87.
3. Ibid.
4. Lucie-Smith, p. 187.
5. Deposition of d'Aulon, Quicherat III, pp. 217–218.
6. Every May 8, the townspeople of Orleans celebrate their liberation from the English with a solemn procession in Joan's honor. They were among the few who held on to the practice even when Joan had fallen in disrepute.
7. The royal deed ennobling her family is still in archives, see Quicherat V, pp. 15–153.
8. Quicherat V, pp. 156–159.
9. March 3, 1431, VI public session.
10. Cagny, *Chronique*, Quicherat IV, p. 33.
11. The closing of the gate at Compiegne has long been considered suspicious. A debate sprung up almost immediately on the matter. Régine Pernoud gives the most convincing account of the event in her latest book, see *Joan of Arc: Her Story*, pp. 231–233.

CHAPTER 10: BEAUREVOIR

1. Henri Debout, *Jeanne d'Arc et les archives anglaises*, Paris, 1895, pp. 19–20.
2. Monstrelet, *Chroniques*, Quicherat IV, p. 387.
3. Quicherat IV, p. 382.
4. See, for instance, Jean Leclerque, François Vandenbrucke, and

Louis Bouyer, *A History of Christian Spirituality II: The Spirituality of the Middle Ages*, p. 519.
5. Morosini, as quoted by Lucie–Smith, p. 207.
6. See Pierre Champion, *On the Trial of Jeanne d'Arc*, in Barrett, p. 487.
7. Cardini, p. 74.
8. See Sackville-West, pp. 280–281 on this point.
9. See Gies, p. 143.
10. Quicherat V, p. 253.
11. Quicherat, *Apercus nouveaux su l'historie de Jeanne d' Arc*, p. 570.

CHAPTER 11: ROUEN: THE PREAMBLE TO THE END

1. Quicherat V, pp. 191–192.
2. Deposition of Guillaume Manchon, Quicherat III, p. 137.
3. Quicherat III, pp. 147–148.
4. Quicherat V, p. 168.
5. *Bourgeois de Paris*, p. 268.
6. Quicherat V, p. 156–159.
7. George Holmes, "Cardinal Beaufort and the Crusade against the Hussites," *English Historical Review*, 349 (Oct. 1973), 721–750.

CHAPTER 12: ROUEN: THE TRIAL

1. Deposition of Guillaume Manchon, Quicherat III, p. 137.
2. Deposition of Jean Massieu, Quicherat III, p. 153.
3. Deposition of Jean Massieu, Quicherat III, p. 153.
4. Pernoud, *Joan of Arc: Her Story*, p. 108.
5. Gies, p. 248.
6. Lucie-Smith, pp. 22–24. The point is Lucie-Smith's premise and gives a psychoanalytic reading of Joan's life and behavior.
7. See, e.g., Lucie-Smith, p. 34: "Yet, in putting on male dress, Joan undoubtedly discovered something that corresponded to a deep-seated need within herself. It was the revelation of a hitherto unknown aspect of her own nature, and having found this, she was never afterwards able to deny it."
8. Karen Sullivan, in Fresh Verdicts on Joan of Arc (ed. Bonnie Wheeler and Charles T. Wood), pp. 265–288.
9. See, for instance, Anne Llewellyn Barstow, *Joan of Arc: Heretic, Mystic, Shaman*.
10. February 21, 1431, I public session.
11. Ibid.
12. February, 24, 1431, III public session.
13. Ibid.

14. Ibid.
15. March 3, 1431, VI public session.
16. Ibid.
17. March 1, 1431, V public session.
18. March 17, 1431, prison session.
19. March 3, 1431, VI public session.
20. February 27, 1431, IV public session. See also February 22, 1431, II public session.
21. As serious as these charges were, however, they too were unfounded. It must be remember that Joan had submitted to the Church Militant on at least two occasions. She had had a small hearing in Chinon, and a three week one in Portiers. The latter commission gave her the official approval of the Church Militant.

There is some evidence that Joan herself took the phrase "Church Militant" to mean Cauchon's inquisition. Isambard de la Pierre later claimed: "During a large part of the trial, when she was questioned about submission to the Church, Joan understood by 'Church' the gathering of judges and assessor there present." See Quicherat II, p. 4.
22. Response to the first of the seventy articles.
23. Deposition of Pierre Miget, Quicherat II, p. 361; deposition of Jean de Mailly, Quicherat III, p. 55; deposition of Jean Marcel, Quicherat III, p. 90.

CHAPTER 13: NATIONS LOST AND FOUND

1. Georges Duby, *France in the Middle Ages 987–1460*, p. 245.
2. Deposition of Dunois, Quicherat III, p. 13; deposition of d'Alençon, Quicherat III, p. 100.
3. Deposition of d'Alençon, Quicherat III, p. 100.
4. See Marina Warner, *Joan of Arc*, p. 159.
5. See Bonnie Wheeler, "Joan of Arc's Sword in the Stone," in *Fresh Verdicts on Joan of Arc*, xi.
6. See Margolis, "The 'Joan Phenomenon' and the French Right," pp. 265–288 on this point.
7. Bourdeilles as quoted by Jane Marie Pinzino, "Speaking of Angels: A Fifteenth-Century Bishop in Defense of Joan of Arc's Mystical Voices," in *Fresh Verdicts on Joan of Arc*, p. 165.
8. March 1, 1431, V public session.
9. March 17, 1431, prison session.
10. March 1, 1431, V public session.
11. March 17, 1431, prison session.
12. See Pierre Champion, *On the Trial of Jeanne d'Arc*, in Barrett, p. 487.
13. Barrett, pp. 165–166.

BIBLIOGRAPHY

Bibliography on Joan of Arc is extensive. The primary sources are the minutes of her Rouen and her rehabilitation trials. There are a number of editions of these minutes. The most consulted are:

Jules Quicherat. *Procès de condemnation et de réhabilitation de Jeanne d'Arc*, dite la Pucelle, Paris, 1841–1849.

Pierre Tisset and Yvonne Lanhers. *Procès de condemnation et de réhabilitation de Jeanne d'Arc*, dite la Pucelle, Paris, 1870.

Pierre Champion. *Procès de condemnation et de réhabilitation de Jeanne d'Arc*, dite la Pucelle, Paris, 1920–1921.

The most complete English translations of the trial proceedings are:

W. P. Barrett. *The Trial of Joan of Arc*, London, 1931.

W.S. Scott. *The Trial of Joan of Arc*, London, 1956.

Regine Pernoud. *The Retrial of Joan of Arc*, New York: Hartcourt, Brace and Co., 1955.

In recent times, a new edition of the trial proceedings has been published by Marina Warner, *The Trial of Joan of Arc*, Evesham: Arthur James, 1996.

In order to facilitate consultation of the minutes, I have chosen to follow W. S. Scott's example and refer the reader to the date of Joan's interrogation, rather than to a specific edition of the minutes of the trial itself. For the rehabilitation readings I have used the Quicherat edition.

There is an inordinate amount of secondary literature on Joan. Listed below are a few of the classical biographies of Joan, a few of the more recent biographies, as well as a selection of novels, critiques, and rereadings of Joan's life and personality. I have attempted to list at least one book for each of the schools of thought on Joan.

Barstow, Anne Llewellyn. *Joan of Arc: Heretic, Mystic, Shaman*, Lewiston/Queenston: Edwin Mellen Press, 1986. The book is an attempt to prove that Joan of Arc was actually involved in the occult. It is a good example of the feminist attempt to reevaluate Joan.

Belloc, Hillaire. *Joan of Arc*, New York: Newman Press, 1998. A brief but beautiful biography of Joan.

Cardini, Franco. *Giovanna d'Arco*, Milan: Mondadori, 1998. One of the most serious recent biographies of Joan written by one of the great contemporary European historians.

Clemens, Samuel. *Joan of Arc*, San Francisco: Ignatius Press, 1990. Mark Twain's tribute to Joan of Arc. He considered it the best of his novels.

Gies, Frances. *Joan of Arc: the Legend and the Reality*, New York: Harper and Row, 1981. This is a solid biography of Joan.

Lucie-Smith, Edward. *Joan of Arc*, New York: W. Norton Co. Inc, 1977. The object of this book is to give a psychoanalytic reading of Joan, and to prove that she was not an authentic visionary. It was well received in England when it was published.

Margolis, Nadia. *Joan of Arc in History, Literature, and Film*, New York: Garland Publishing Inc., 1990. The most complete bibliography of works on Joan available in print in the English language.

Marcantel, Pamela. *Army of Angels*, New York: St. Martin's press. This is a new novel on Joan. Its most surprising characteristic is that it attempts to reconstruct the dialogue between Joan and her voices.

Michelet, Jules. *Joan of Arc*, Ann Arbor: University of Michigan Press, 1957. A reprint of one of the classical biographies on Joan.

Pernoud, Regine. *Joan of Arc: by Herself and her Witnesses*, Lanham MD, Scarborough House, 1994. Pernoud's best biography of Joan. Pernoud tells Joan's story through the trial minutes.

———. *Joan of Arc: Her Story*, New York: St. Martin's Press, 1999. Pernoud's last book. It is well worth reading.

Poole, Josephine. *Joan of Arc*, New York: Knopf, 1998. This is a children's book. The illustrations are beautiful.

Sackville-West, Victoria. *Saint Joan of Arc*, New York-Garden City: Doubleday, Doran and Co., 1936. A classic biography of Joan and a beautiful book.

Scott, W.S. *Jeanne d'Arc: Her Life, Death and the Myth*, New York: Barnes and Noble, 1974. This is another classic biography of Joan.

Stanley, Dianne. *Joan of Arc*, New York: Marrow Junior, 1998. Another children's book, and lovely.

Sullivan, Karen. *Fresh Verdicts on Joan of Arc* (ed. Bonnie Wheeler and Charles T. Wood), New York: Garland Publishing, Inc., 1996.

Trask, William. Ed. *Joan of Arc: In Her Own Words*, New York: Turtle Point, 1996. A compilation of Joan's words, drawn from the trial minutes.

Warner, Marina. *Joan of Arc*, New York: Knopf, 1981. The book is an analysis of Joan of Arc and her cult.

INDEX